# WHAT IT FEELS LIKE

By the same author:

*Why I am Not a Farmer*
*A Paddock in His Head*
*A Tight Circle*
*Travelling Through the Family*
*Small Town Soundtrack*
*The Lowlands of Moyne*
*Walk Like a Cow (memoir)*
*Feldspar*

# WHAT IT FEELS LIKE

## New and selected poems

# BRENDAN RYAN

RECENT
WORK
PRESS
2015-2025
10 YEARS OF POETRY

What It Feels Like: New and Selected Poems
Recent Work Press
Canberra, Australia

Copyright © Brendan Ryan, 2025

ISBN: 9781763670136 (paperback)

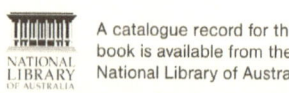

A catalogue record for this book is available from the National Library of Australia

All rights reserved. This book is copyright. Except for private study, research, criticism or reviews as permitted under the Copyright Act, no part of this book may be reproduced, stored in a retrieval system, or transmitted in any form by any means without prior written permission. Enquiries should be addressed to the publisher.

Cover image: © Brendan Ryan, 2025
Cover design: Recent Work Press
Set by Recent Work Press

recentworkpress.com
10 YEARS OF POETRY

*In memory of*
*Frank Ryan*
*29/11/1936-14/10/2024*

# Contents

Self-portrait     1

## WHY I AM NOT A FARMER

| | |
|---|---|
| Why I am not a farmer | 5 |
| The blessing | 7 |
| Eel conditions | 9 |
| Losing to the cow | 10 |
| Corrugated iron | 12 |
| Morning after | 14 |
| Argyle St | 16 |
| Country parents in town | 17 |
| The best day in his life | 18 |
| The benefits of a rotary dairy | 20 |
| Milk fever | 24 |
| Return to the Western District | 26 |
| The killer | 29 |

## A PADDOCK IN HIS HEAD

| | |
|---|---|
| I know, I know | 33 |
| Catholic daydreams | 34 |
| What it feels like | 35 |
| A beautiful ruin | 36 |
| Farm boys | 37 |
| Gravel stories | 38 |
| A job to do | 39 |
| Permanent as can be | 40 |
| She lets go | 42 |
| Cow with paralysis | 44 |
| The view | 45 |
| Catching a train to intimacy | 48 |
| The paddock with the big tree in it | 50 |
| Maternity paddock | 51 |
| A paddock in his head | 53 |
| Tower Hill | 54 |

| | |
|---|---|
| Uncles and aunties | 56 |
| Hayseeds | 58 |
| A walk to the supermarket | 59 |
| Teenage riot | 61 |
| A breather | 63 |
| Back roads, local roads | 66 |

## A TIGHT CIRCLE

| | |
|---|---|
| Woman wearing a hairnet | 73 |
| Talking to auntie | 74 |
| A tight circle | 76 |
| Factory boys | 78 |
| Back streets | 80 |
| Choppers | 82 |
| On chook time | 83 |

## TRAVELLING THROUGH THE FAMILY

| | |
|---|---|
| Blister country | 87 |
| A dark place | 88 |
| Abattoir sonnet | 89 |
| The killing work | 90 |
| Summer grasses | 91 |
| Vacant blocks | 92 |
| Cowshit | 93 |
| Man on the gate | 94 |
| Travelling through the family | 95 |
| Mother and daughter | 97 |
| Equilibrium | 98 |
| True confessions | 99 |
| Tour of duty | 101 |
| Philip Hodgins | 102 |
| Late summer light | 104 |
| *from* Driving sonnets | 105 |

## SMALL TOWN SOUNDTRACK

| | |
|---|---|
| Outsider pastoral | 109 |
| To do list | 111 |

| | |
|---|---|
| Grounded angels | 113 |
| Dairy farmers at the beach | 115 |
| Sign of peace | 117 |
| Small town pastoral | 118 |
| What the night gives | 119 |
| Across the universe | 120 |
| Inner beat | 121 |
| Ecklin | 123 |
| Hurtle | 124 |
| Camellias | 125 |
| At fifty | 127 |
| She talks of a future | 128 |
| Cows in India | 129 |
| The politics that will drive my own ageing | 131 |

## THE LOWLANDS OF MOYNE

| | |
|---|---|
| She was a Mugavin | 135 |
| A father's silences | 136 |
| The lowlands of Moyne | 138 |
| The violin player | 140 |
| Farmer's wife | 143 |
| Everything becomes metaphor | 145 |
| Hinterlands | 146 |
| The things they carry | 148 |
| Men I have worked with | 150 |
| Ampilatwatja | 152 |
| Driving with the West MacDonnells | 154 |
| Driving to debating | 156 |
| Forgiven | 157 |
| Heifer wearing a fence post | 158 |
| Dehorning | 159 |
| The smell of a paddock | 161 |
| Home | 163 |

## FELDSPAR

| | |
|---|---|
| Feldspar | 167 |
| The parents | 169 |
| Sonnets for a mother | 171 |
| Watching the news | 174 |
| What I return to and miss | 176 |

| | |
|---|---|
| The potato bag needle | 178 |
| Driving through mallee towns | 180 |
| Bleached paddocks | 181 |
| Language of rubs | 182 |
| Between the pen and the roundabout | 183 |
| Between a paddock and a hayshed | 184 |
| What we did to each other | 185 |
| Taking it slow | 188 |
| Turning my back on Australians overseas | 190 |
| Midnight Oil at Mt Duneed | 191 |

# NEW POEMS

| | |
|---|---|
| Distances | 195 |
| Roaming | 197 |
| Weather | 199 |
| The Simpson twin tub | 201 |
| Fifth avenue | 203 |
| Dreams a daughter lets slip | 205 |
| Parenting days | 206 |
| Rats | 207 |
| Three walks | 208 |
| Visitors | 209 |
| Joan Eardley | 210 |
| Summer's abandonment | 212 |
| The snaking accuracy of cow trails | 213 |
| Storm cell | 215 |
| Hard worker | 216 |
| The boys | 217 |
| Archway | 218 |
| Fifteen dollars | 220 |
| Circle work | 222 |
| Inheritance | 223 |
| There, there | 224 |
| Blown showers | 225 |
| Walking the cattle track | 227 |
| Caring pantoum | 228 |
| Drover boy | 230 |
| The roster | 231 |
| Coolum Beach boardwalk | 233 |
| Finding pieces of my father | 234 |
| And still the wind moans | 235 |
| Barmah | 236 |

# Self-portrait

The sweep of grey skies
baling twine snagged on barbed wire,
the squelch of rubber boots
trees I planted, knocked about by weather.

The roar of wind is the roar of memory.
I'm walking with my head down, thoughts racing
feet stumbling over hoof prints.
These paddocks have made me,
shaped the way I look at mud around gateways.
The windmill has collapsed, yet the smell of mud
endures like worms coming out after rain.
Sun rising over the ridge of a ploughed paddock
imprints my shadow, extending it.
I watch myself walk ahead

into paddocks and more poems.
Half-succeeding in understanding yet
knowing my limits, self-doubt increasing with age
with rage, wind along the bush boundary
confirms this. A nagging, almost a toothache
propels me, some insatiable inner urge
that won't be satisfied. Sisyphus had nothing on this—
pulled to the farm I grew up on
walking through paddocks I can't live with.

The milking herd nods along a rutted track.
Thistles and tussocks on the low flats around drains.
Each image is selected, cropped, put to work in memoryland:
where somebody else spikes the round bales,
loses thirty thousand with a drop in milk price
the knackery charging to pick up dead cows,

my niece milking the first herd by 4:30am.
I'm a visitor with a vested interest.
These poems have made me

aware of my place in a large family—
always trying to be noticed, connected,
at the mercy of memory
hoping to bring these paddocks alive.
Writing poems has become something I do—
essential as making coffee, necessary
as my father returning to get his son's cows in.
They make strange things common,
a way of living within a piece of land.
I walk these paddocks and the wind cleans me out.

# WHY I AM NOT A FARMER

# Why I am not a farmer

I live in the city
without a windmill, electric fence or bull
to admire.
The country is made of things
newsreaders are reluctant to mention:
The presence of a priest amongst Catholic wives
carloads of farmers drinking themselves naked down back roads
teenage sons driving into trees
or catapulting through the fog
to smash their skulls on a rock.
                        Working dogs
are shot by farmers
as their use-by date expires.
Dead cows are skinned, boiled and squeezed
into Pal tins. Old bulls die of envy.

Mostly it is the talk of leaving
that keeps you in the country—
your big ideas pulled back into line
by the gun of a Sunday barrel
where girlfriends are handed the keys
men use their boots
to scrape paddocks in the dust
and spit between their teeth
with the credibility hobby farmers dream of.

But you can only reach inside a cow
to turn a calf around,
squeegee the shit from a dairy
turn away from the swollen cheekbones
of a neighbour's wife
for so long.

I was raised on questions
my father couldn't answer.

I remember
I always dreamed of freeways.

# The blessing

Two shooters call in at the dairy
wanting to plaster a few foxes.
'Last time, there were two

that gave us a beating.
Today—we're ready for war.'
'Yeah, go ahead,' my father shouts,

watching a bottle of calcium drain
through a needle into the stomach
of a prostrate, fevery cow. Through

the railings, the shooters pick out
my city clothes, the shocked expressions
of friends keeping their distance

from various bits of afterbirth,
the shit-splattered pressure hose,
as they discover what country people do

on Sundays. 'But I'll have two bob
on the foxes again,' my father adds,
which is all the shooters need

to smile, back away, rattling change
in their pockets; reminding me
how warm a bullet feels

when you've been rubbing it all day
as my father concentrates
on saving this cow

by kicking it in the ribs,
which is a type of country blessing.

# Eel conditions

Cows kept their distance
as we carried old broom handles with three filed prongs
down to the creek.
For hunters with no heritage
we had learned from the snags and reeds
when to send our spears home
into the dark, wriggling flesh.
Depending on what our mothers had cooked the night before
we'd cut off its head
and throw the rest into the bucket we used for feeding calves.
But if we'd been having eel all week
our knives were put away
and jokes entered a new dimension.
With the eel writhing at our feet
we'd snap off branches,
pull out the cricket bats we'd been carrying
and bash the eel's head to smithereens.
A kind of bloodlust
it seemed to bring us together
as we split the skin and pulverised the grass around its flopping head.
But like going to the Hot Rods was really to crack onto girls
bashing eels was only part of the joke.
The real pleasure was in getting out of the house
away from parents and milking cows,
returning to those patches in the creek
where we pitted our memories
against the wind shivering upstream
and read the creek for eel conditions.
At fourteen, it was something to do.

# Losing to the cow

My brother and I change our grip on the slimy rope
and pull as if we are hauling
our childhood into view—

stormy nights lost to cows with ruptured wombs,
cows licking their calves with two feet of afterbirth
hanging to the ground.

My father loops the rope around his waist
pushes his foot against a rail
and leans back like an anchorman.

The calf stares down at our faces
straining against its weight.
My fingers slip on the mucus

and for a moment it seems we are losing
to the cow,
being pulled forward by something larger

than the shoulders of a calf,
as if the cow is teasing us
withholding our history

until my brother's D. Ms are splattered with blood,
my 501s flecked with the shit
I used to comb from my hair.

But the smell of the dairy
is all my brother and I need
to know of childhood,

and the way a calf spills toward you
before hitting the concrete.
'Another stinkin' bull'

with its tongue hanging at our feet,
already it seems to know
its position in this life.

# Corrugated iron

'these are the late rains
the river flats need
for the green pick to shoot'

Tonight the world is anchored
to the wings of a roofing nail.
I move away from sleep
and doubt if I'll ever return.
Sheets of corrugated iron murmur and sigh
threaten to take flight
from hours of soft pummelling.

I chase day old calves through driving rain
away from the pit of their mother's eye,
and with a sledgehammer
draw blood from those underweight and unsaleable.

The cowyard air
tattoos my forearms
in bands of stained clover.

Three hundred Hereford steers bellow through the house
looking for a bag of blood-stained horns.
With blood spurting from jagged stumps
and pink nostrils flared
they upend the kitchen table, shit on our beds.
Spooked into a rampage
they have trampled the landscape
between dairy and house—
the drifting garden,
walking tracks we scuff a connection to—
all buried under the hooves of cattle.

Beneath a row of withered gums
the collapsed skin of a bull
slips from the teeth
of a ribcage.

Nearby an assortment of bones
left by crows, a stray eagle,
cattle dogs in their wilder moments.
the skull, dragged to the side
records sunlight passing through two hollow wounds.

A pillow of dust cushions the ebbing storm.
The house sits in the palm of domestic silence.
As the ghost of a wind shakes rain from cypress trees
I trace my skin with a pencil of sleep
and walk the furrows of a ploughed paddock.
Each ridge forms a relief map
to the fragmenting bed of iron curling like old skin
from rain-soaked battens.

# Morning after

I stand with my father
in the tyre marks of fire trucks
looking across burnt paddocks.
Paddocks he has walked in his head, in his dreams.
The same paddocks we have talked into arguments.

The past is scorched, but its heat
rises through my work boots.
My father shakes his head
scuffs his boots in the ashes of a fence post,
'You wouldn't credit it.'

A skinless calf hobbles from a drain.
Whispering beneath tangled fencing wire
the husk of a strainer post.
The strip of bush I explored as a child
has been left in black slivers.
There is a cemetery quiet my father
won't admit. He spits, rattles change
in his pockets as smoke enters
our clothes, skin

a bulldozer fills a pit with burnt cows.
Their skin has been toasted the same grey colour,
are they Jersey, Friesian or Hereford?
They fall from the bulldozer's bucket in clumps
ten at a time, sideways, headfirst thudding
into place amongst the flies.
      Some cows miss the hole
and land broken-necked, half-in
half-out, forcing the operator
to scoop them up and start over again.

A siren wails through charred gum trees
lining Heathmarsh Road.
Beneath the dirt, tree roots and peat bogs
smoulder and grow. Everything
we've ever leant against
has been shelled and scattered.

# Argyle St

The sky fractures like a windscreen
the blue Mobil Mart sign keeps the intersection alive.
Somewhere a tram, dance music.
A council worker weaves
out of a pub doorway.
The idea of living here

amongst slabs of 70s red brick
where developers slip you 300 to move out
and walk away from your vegie patch
making plans for concrete, fake grass

in a landscape of reclaimed mansions
where a man walks the street reading *Son of Rosemary,*
others shuffle in pyjamas past traffic jams—
ciggies dangling, eyes glazed, talking to trees
making milk bar owners nervous.

I meet my neighbours at the clothesline
the small talk falls between us
like pegs in the basket.

Nights glow in passing planes
the honeycomb light of the Commission flats
towering above the antennas, chimneys,
a rubber tree concealing a shopping trolley
and our compost bin watched over by cats

who track my movements in this fibro sunroom
where I'm often at sea leaning against a door jamb
that's seen better days, with the changes
sweeping in from the Bay
the way a memory leaves you in its wake.

# Country parents in town

They walk the streets
arm in arm
to the memory of Marriage Encounter
proving love lasts away from the farm.

They keep a sharp eye
for exit ramps, the nearest church
cars mounting the footpath
and ply us with bulk groceries
from a butter factory's general store.

They wear wallets in their top pockets
and prefer a thermos in the car
to a cappuccino at Southbank.
Theirs is a hostile imagination.

# The best day in his life

There wasn't anybody to disturb him.
All morning he had been with the radio
listening for his son's ute in the driveway.
Light forgetful showers blew through his raked leaves
the way his son was throwing money around
on new cars, vats, a rotary dairy.
He thought of the get-up-and-go
his son lacked on Sunday mornings
and how, so much lately he had been counting on
those late nights—
the job of fetching his son's milkers under dawn skies.

Now in the afternoon, the grass still wet, the son at the footy
he takes the tractor into the river paddock
feeds some hay to the heifers, then hooks
the smudgers up to the tractor.
He tows those lengths of railway iron
round the paddock, through tussocks and ferns,
the noise of the tractor easing him into memory.
He drives in a twisted position
to follow the scars the smudger makes,
to smell the paddock taking shape.
Every now and then he glances ahead
to check the tractor's path, and sees his father:
a doom-and-gloom-man
who used to sit around and watch things.

But like the heifers chewing their hay
he knows these paddocks by their drains
mounds of old fence lines,
the distance between troughs.
He knows that by kicking the dirt around on top

some green pick might rise from beneath.
The heifers might hold their condition
for another couple of weeks.
There wasn't anybody to disturb him.

# The benefits of a rotary dairy

A rotary dairy allows you to hold your head up
in local conversations
to milk double the amount of cows

in the time it takes a paddock to breathe.
The secret to success is feed in the bail
a 10,000 litre vat that has learnt to wash itself

thirty-two cows going around on a platform.
As one cow is being head-butted onto it
another cow is stepping back off.

Like clockwork, 300 cows in two hours.
In the old walk-through, half the time was spent
stepping in amongst them, squeezing between

their pregnant stomachs, whacking their rumps
with a piece of poly pipe, as you hunted for that
undershot Guernsey who likes the third bail.

Invariably, you copped a hoof print on the toe
of your rubber boot and were pushed aside
by an unmilked heifer bolting for her life

but who ended up in the bail, nervous and unaware
of your faith in leg ropes. Back then, most cows
had names. You knew their history by the type of knot

you tied their outside ankle back with.
A double knot for the heifers and mongrel choppers
who kicked in a three-foot arc and kept you wary

a single knot for old Jerseys like Mary, who dragged her teats
in the mud and stood in the bail meditating
before nail holes of light in the door.

And because she gave twice as much as any Friesian
was given an extra yank of the feed cord. The wooden
levers we pulled the doors open with were shaped

by water-softened hands. I kept an instinctual distance
from their smooth shit-stained handles whenever
an impatient Friesian banged the stumps of her horns

against the door. But the cows rarely leapt into daylight
with their machines on. Most times I was kept busy
running between bails with a stooped back

squatting to pick up the machines from the mud
while my father leant against a roof support
softened by his shoulder listening to the saleyard prices

before turning the radio off when the music came on.
All that's left now of the walk-through is the concrete
of the holding yard. Four square metres mapped by cracks

and sloping into a drain that fed the vegie garden I cordoned
off from the bulls by an electric wire. Every Saturday morning
before footy, it was my job to squee gee the yard—

pushing the shit of 140 cows into a one-foot opening.
In time, I knew that holding yard like the pockets
of the footy oval, and would clean it dreaming

of rising above the pack for a screamer as Casey Kasem
let me know who was down from one on American Top 40.
Now the drain is blocked by weeds

and the holding yard has become a pen for new bull calves
before they're sold and turned into pet food.
Anybody will tell you walk-throughs

are a thing of the past—a place
where memory and lies curdle.
Down here, where the herd's

bad breath keeps the weather out
and the cows circulate
like parts on an assembly line

the radio still crackles through a playlist that stopped at 1985.
In that nine-a-side pit my father opened up
and I learned to keep opinions to myself.

The whole family would be summoned to the yard
for important news, warnings were followed by stories
and things I never heard him talk about

when there wasn't a cow in sight. In that corridor
between the cows, we'd pass each other
in a kind of trance, spitting in the mud

our jobs determined by experience—I opened the steel gate
he got out into the herd selecting with his poly pipe,
all the while chanting—'the easiest job you ever had.'

Although the herringbone was an improvement
on the walk-through, my sisters and mother
rarely milked again. Our family roles were decided

studied and memorised from an early age—
boys in the dairy, girls in the kitchen.
By the time my elder brother started dyeing his hair blue

I could milk 160 cows on my own
moving up and down the pit to *I'm Stranded*
a song the radio station was ignorant of

as was my father whose back was being shortened
in a Massey Ferguson seat bouncing over the ridges
of a paddock that hadn't been ploughed before.

These days every cow is a number with an A.I history.
Religious discussions are no longer possible.
The roar of the engine is absolutely modern.

My father's office has been replaced by a series of nods
frowns, the occasional stubby being passed around.
There is no time for paddock views

while waiting for a big Friesian to finish.
No time to give a careful eye
to the first run entering the night paddock.

Looking out over the overflow drain
I see things as they really are—
a cattle dog tearing into a dead calf.

You push a button and the herd shuffles toward you.

# Milk fever

Ibis' picking in mud
heifers crowding around to sniff my jeans

a fence post being banged in paddocks away
beneath the pine trees, a dead cow

her stomach torn apart by dogs and foxes
wind arguing with a eucalypt plantation

my father whistling from the check-out
to collect ten kids in Target

he feeds the springers pellets before they calve
last year six cows were lost to milk fever

these paddock spaces are pockets of memory
Mt Warrnambool caught in the drizzle

a cow decaying amongst mossy rocks
a dog's instinct for killing snakes

shopping on a Wednesday with 20 cents
my nerves shot by the hum of an electric fence

the isolation of the back river flats
dark water stroked by reeds

the white plank fence that sagged around the house
barbed wire fences bowed by falling trees

wood from the wheelbarrow outside the back door
Mum pregnant, on her knees, mopping the floor

dead crows and sheep skins draped over the chook shed walls
dust clouds pulling eyes to the car coming down the road

wind rising from the hole in the floor beside my bed
where the machinery shed was, where the diesel tank was

walking along the bush track
I was on edge between boundary fences

stumbling through hoofprints,
reassured by shotgun cartridges

my first drink in a hotel was a raspberry
on a high stool beside my father

I saw neighbours grinning out of the dark
shadows approaching the frosted glass

the views of paddocks and Occupation Lane
are the same, it's where I'm looking from that's changed

# Return to the Western District

Driving through the Stony Rises at night
you enter a purple light
which sits above the paddocks
pulls you into swamps,
slanted pig sheds, ferns rising
out of dumped windscreens.
The only things that seem to move
are rocks slipping from dry-stone fences.
These are paddocks haunted by their ordering
where the massacre years pass with Bunyips into myth,
our colonial history.

With each sweeping bend
or five-mile stretch
the Western District darkness opens up
secrets, histories you don't hear about.
The paddocks close in.
Every farmhouse throws a familiar shadow.
Car lights coming down a side road
fail to reassure me against these vast, unwritten plains.
And all the things like Indigenous Australians
my parents wouldn't talk about at the kitchen table
suddenly seem irrelevant in the overtaking lane.

This is the road Nanna travelled
to see a daughter dying of TB.
Too poor to catch a train she hitched rides
with trucks, then six weeks later
caught a ride back with the hearse,
her daughter keeping quiet behind her.

To fill in the silences on long trips
my parents would say a decade of the rosary.
Dad, in his monotone mantra
ran words into each other—
*hailMaryfullagraceLordiswthee.*
We were a family resigning to their own rhythm
and Mum interjecting—'pray up, I can't hear you'
      —our holiday treat from kneeling on lino tiles.
I sank into my window seat
mumbling responses to the weeds
spaces between fence posts.

Passing the derestriction signs outside Terang
is passing into the grainy light of an unfinished dream.
Faces, paddocks, voices out of focus
and for a moment I'm driving underwater.
There is the paddock where the Drive-In was
here are the two chimneys left from a bushfire.
Down to Yaloak Creek bridge
up past Johnny Ryans, Meades.
These are the names a city can't supply.
These are the histories I'm stuck with.

A small town's gift to the world
may be a card night that stops people
from sitting around and staring at themselves.
Like footy streamers tied to white posts
my parents keep themselves busy
avoiding doctors
looking up from ad breaks
to photos on the wall.

Here where legends are invented each weekend
free beer on Christmas morning
brings a farming community together—
teenage mothers and red-cheeked bachelors,

dope smokers and relief milkers,
the nicknames of last year's Premiership side
decorate the bar.

Each time I return
certain objects are caught:
green algae in a water trough
a cattle track rising out of river flats.
So much slips from that first glance
I can't pick up everything that falls.
In the quiet paddocks
that have been shut up for hay
all I can hear are sirens, Punt Rd traffic.

I shake a loose fence post and the earth squelches.

# The killer

There is a killing spot. A permanent patch of dirt below a cypress tree, its branches cut back to open the view for the mother washing the red-spotted chopping board she uses for sheep's liver. Most times the kill is brief, doesn't take more than a minute. The hardest part is bunching the sheep or killers as they are called into a fence corner and pouncing on the ewe with the killing fear in its eyes. This ewe is usually the fattest in a cluster of wethers and lambs. After those few near misses, grazed knees and the dogs have finally chased the sheep in the right direction, drag the killer toward the cypress tree while its cousins flee in terror. It is a blood sport requiring a certain amount of skill to flip the sheep on its side, kneel, swing your knee into its back and shove the head into the dirt. Don't worry about the legs or the bleating— the sound of a knife being scraped on a stone quietens things down. Pull the sheep's head back so your other knee fits snug in the crook of its neck. It doesn't hurt to relax your weight on the sheep's back, give the dogs a clout if they're nipping at the hooves—it's the least you can do to give the sheep some peace. Take your knife, prise open the lice-riddled folds and with the ease of slicing oven-baked bread cut through until you feel the neck bones. Make sure the blood needles out away from you— flies love blood and Omo only smudges the memory. Now the kill is almost over, your one act of grace remains to be done. Pull the sheep's head back against your knee until the neck bones crack, the eyeballs swivel and the gagging stops. Stand back, give the flies some room and with a cigarette watch the nerves kick in those final thrashing moments.

# A PADDOCK IN HIS HEAD

# I know, I know

the horizon by the back roads which lead to it
and when we start selling mushrooms in May
our neighbours up the road will follow

my brothers and I know which bull we can't trust
we play sock footy down the hall
as the radio gives the day's footy scores
from Bessiebelle

each night our house is hugged
by the wind
each night our paddocks are interrupted
by lights from the neighbour's dairy
today everything hangs askew

I lay back on the super bags
listening
to dogs dragging their chains
over half-buried bones

Mum walks out into the paddock
hurls tea leaves down the drain
we empty the toilet bucket into

some days I lay under the house
listening to the scrape
of chairs on lino

some days are rosaries that never end.

# Catholic daydreams

Lost in language
my brothers and sisters
flick food scraps at each other

as the circular rhythms
of lead and response
echo across paddocks,

the kitchens of large families
humming with Hail Marys
the wind, like a semaphore

tunnels down chimneys.
My father's dairy farming fingers
slip down the beads

as if each bead was a grip
on the Joyful Mystery
of ten children charging through

the Hail Holy Queen,
the tempo picking up
according to what was on TV.

Yet after we had finished
we would often remain kneeling
heads down, studying the lino

and those catholic daydreams.

# What it feels like

It is two fathers punching each other in the footy sheds
shadows extending over the river flats

over the bachelor nursing a long neck on his porch
over the epileptic twisting on the mechanic's floor.

It is a chorus of crows in the red gums by the river.
It is a woman avoiding loose gravel on the road to her lover.

It is the sound of water foaming up in paddocks
it is the scrape of hoof prints on the cattle track.

It is the one finger wave above the steering wheel
a row of fox skins stretched along a fence,

a farmer growing up once his parents have died
three unmarried sisters avoiding eyes on their way out of church.

It is a gust of wind shuddering through a row of eucalypts
teenage lovers divorcing twenty years later.

My rubber boots sinking into family sayings
a man taking to his car with an axe.

# A beautiful ruin

School holidays
we take to the piano with axes
smashing the keys, the ivories
destroying what is beautiful.
A worn upright left by previous owners
receiving the brunt of weather
facing west on our front verandah.
A thing to be tinkered with
passed over, a distraction through the minutes.
It was never going to make money for the farm
or fill our empty cupboards.
It was a beautiful thing to ruin
to hammer into pieces, to jump on
stamp on, to give our holidays reason.
We had boredom to burn
the paddocks were another world
of jobs and teasing distances
enclosing us like our neighbours' far-off voices.
We wanted to damage something closer
to home.
We stormed inside, triumphant
breathless as angels, pushing and shoving.
'We bashed up the piano Mum.'
Her face went red
as she rose from the newspapers
spread out across the damp lino
of the newly washed kitchen floor.
She chased us with a tea towel.
Her voice began to quiver and screech.
It was a beautiful thing to ruin.

# Farm boys

You can see their utes pulling dust toward the highway
smell the Brut, blue jeans
pressed by their mother
the night's milking shadowing their palms.

You can tell by the way they arrive
at a decent hour
support the bar with steady conversation
add weight to the walls
watching girls they cannot talk to.

You can tell by the way they drink
without getting their lips wet
how they listen after a handshake
study their boots as a woman passes
and five beers later, stories of their father.

You might remember them at the hamburger van
tall as hay sheds, still listening
to your opinions, the note
of your girlfriend's car they will memorise
until the sound of their tyres punishing gravel
becomes the night
driving itself home.

# Gravel stories

He was turning into his gateway
when he was struck from behind.

Fog had stolen the road
barbed wire couldn't hold back the quiet

or the farmer
trying to believe what the fog revealed:

his brother dead and a neighbour
shaking against the side of a car.

Road accidents, suicides, careless deaths
a district catches its breath

as memories trail a family's name:
his son getting through the fence with a shotgun

her parents cleaned up by a milk tanker.
Talk around the kitchen table

slows down to a stare out the window
a shaking of the head, questions.

They sat a stubby on the grave
of a footballer everybody knew

then drank the afternoon to his name.
Somewhere near the Drive-in

they rolled and she flew
like a story itching to be told.

# A job to do

Hitting a crippled calf on the head
with the blunt end of an axe
because the calf won't survive
past a few days, it won't fetch
anything from the calf buyers
and I know Dad is going to check on me
this is just something I have to do.
Before I pick up the axe handle
I look around the paddocks
to see if anybody is watching
and could they talk me out of this—
a crippled calf between my legs
and my father's words.
I pick up the axe
remembering how my father swings it,
those times I had to look away
stomping up from the drain
with an axe in his hands.
The dull thud is a blow
I know is successful.
The calf's tongue is hanging out
my heart is thumping
as if something has been added
transferred from the sudden jolt
to the calf's head. I step back
utterly alone as my father was
looking for the next job.
At ten I know what it is like to kill.

# Permanent as can be

Foggy morning, in the darkness
I hear the sound of a motorbike
far off, yet personal, my brother checking
his springers for mishaps, cows cast
into ditches unable to get up, a new-born calf
hobbling through the frost, searching
eventually sucking from another cow.
I've been awake all-night waiting
to be out here watching shadows lift
from pine trees around the old farmhouse—
our former neighbour's house, one
we rented out, brothers and sisters lived in
now the mice have it and a web of memories
becomes currency, like a story told from ten
different perspectives. It's in need of a paint job
yet its place on this hill seems permanent as can be.
I can only remain in it long enough to pass through
note the upended bed, tinnies in the corner.
Walking over a frosted paddock at dawn
is walking into a lunar landscape,
another world where thistles are snap frozen
their position unmoved for days. The closest
these paddocks will get to snow, the chill
on my cheeks has the bite of London
of waiting for a night bus at dawn,
then riding through blinking suburbs
other passengers nodding off or still
yabbering from the night before.
Here, frost is uneventful as a river
still from a lack of winter rains
red algae coating the surface.
A band of mist sits above a fence post

like a mirage, elevated, temporary
as the spirits of clubbers hoarding the back seats
on the night bus harrumphing down narrow lanes
the mood dropping as they clamber off—
'cheers, nice one geezer.'
A band of warmth as I sidle past
a cypress plantation, trees I planted
with my other brother, a warm Spring day
or was it summer? A flock of sparrows
flees from within, throwing me backwards
as if I have been caught up by memory,
or the day, 'truly happening' as calves
bawling in a dairy, steam rising
from a pile of fresh cow shit.
Three super bins stand on a ridge
ultra, alien, like something out of Star Wars
ready to stride out across the frost.
'Uphill' there are rumblings in a quarry
traffic streams along the Princes Highway.
I walk down to the river flats
toward a tree that has lain over
spread its canopy of branches like an umbrella.
It seems to suggest something laconic as shelter.

# She lets go

Her hand in mine
she walks looking back
to all the bright colours—
'that's a funny man.'
She says what she feels
and teaches me what I thought I used to know.
The warmth of her hand
the sense that she will never let go,
even though her body
is twisting back to examine
a piece of glass with writing on it.
I have jobs to do:
the ATM, the bookshop, the car.
Her grip tightens
as people navigate father and daughter,
as if we were a reedy outcrop in a river
separated from traffic
and Wednesday shopping day
when I met my mother, here
under the T & G corner.
Insistent memories that I cannot trust.
Was Dad at the pub or the saleyards?
Her hand begins to tug.
This is the place I was picked in broad daylight.
Three men having fun with a country teenager.
After they had shuffled away, laughing
an older woman walking beside me
snapped, 'you should've hit them back
It's disgraceful, a boy your size.'
She walked off leaving me cut down to size
and still my daughter trusts me
to guide her along

when really, I am hanging on
out of fear, out of love.
Nearby, laps are being hung.
Somebody's doof music is another person's flashback.
My daughter's questions are random accidents
in a game of pretend
where I am Amy, Morgan, or Lulu
being pulled toward a teddy display in a chemist window
where she lets go, she lets go.

# Cow with paralysis

Her bag leg is folded up beneath her
you can see the desperation in her eyes.
We know it's helpless

the other cows have abandoned her.
She was trying to calve
when something went inside her.

She was in the moo-mobile for two days
just hanging there, her feet
touching the grass so she could eat.

When we let her down
she flopped to the ground.
It's like shooting a horse

she's fit and healthy in every other way.
If you stand in front of her, she'll thrash
and moan, turn nasty like a prisoner.

I've never seen an eye possess so much anger
now she'll go to the dead cow man.
I've seen his truck turning off the highway

loaded five high on a good day.
Herefords and Jerseys ballooned and spiking the sky
forcing a line of cars to hurriedly overpass.

His business is necessary as death—
he can afford to be friendly, unkempt.
Who wants the job of the dead cow man?

# The view

The view through the kitchen window
was to a playroom that was rarely used.
Toys and dusty photo albums were stuffed
in boxes. The chipboard floor was littered
with blocks and crayons. A child's pram

was upended in a corner. We only went in there
to get away from it all, except it was like
playing in a glass bowl. My mother's life
was spent glancing through the kitchen window
to washing lines, the tank stand and cows

filing up the track. I came in from the dairy
checked the biscuit tin, as I still do,
and asked, 'what's for tea?' The biscuit tin
was a talisman bringing wealth and promise
each Wednesday after shopping. All the tins

and cupboards full, my mother grilled sausages.
I fought with my brothers for the best cream cakes.
I watched *Get Smart* pretending our family was rich
and ate like this every night. My mother hid the biscuit tin
beneath her bed.

It was my turn to empty the scraps bucket.
The chook pen was littered with orange peels.
Occasionally I would read the dirt to discover
last week's meals. Old sheep skins
were draped over the chicken-wire walls.

A dead crow that my father had shot
was wedged between the wires. Each time I woke

to the cawing around the house,
that crow's face in the chicken wire returned.
Dead animals were commonplace on our farm:

we killed our sheep, drowned unwanted kittens,
cows broke hips slipping in the mud
calves died in birth—'but you get that.'
Like the smell my father brought home in the car
when he worked at the knackery in 1975.

The dairy engine purred through our nights
like a soundtrack to the stars blinking
through the darkness. My brother and I
fed the calves with white buckets illuminated
by a rising moon. The milk was straight from the vat

as it was for us, except we added hot water
for the calves. The warm milk ran off the back
of my hands as I thought about a night
in front of the fire. Whoosh! The button
was pressed to stop the engine.

My father's voice, singular in the dark
muttered towards us. 'Shut the gate, tie up the dogs,'
his rubber boots clomping on the gravel.
Tea coincided with the ABC News.
It was a free-for-all. Ten children

stealing potatoes, licking their plates
legs being kicked beneath the table. Dead arms
and arguments that went too far. Five people
crammed onto a red stool. We fought over chairs
over who would do the washing up

as my mother began to pile the day's washing
my father fell asleep with his mouth open.

The TV raged on. Chairs were pushed before
the crackling fire. There was always somebody
warming their calves, 'blocking the heat.'

My mother would never go to bed. Little jobs
kept her running between rooms. When she sat down
I'd trace my fingers around the fireplace grouting
and listen to her talk and look into the hot coals.
A quiet space at the end of the day, 'when I finally

get to sit down.' We'd lean back, hands
supporting our heads, staring at the pens, badges
and ear tags for cows on the mantle-piece.
A remembrance card for a local boy
lay curled and faded beside the grandfather clock.

The phone rarely disturbed us.
My father's abrupt 'hullo' kept us on edge
as we waited to discover who he was talking to.
After tea, the lounge was a space to wrestle in,
play concerts with tennis racquets, my sisters sang

into hairbrushes. The lounge room walls
were thin ply board held together by strips
of two be one. It seems a miracle that nobody
went through them. Yet they were the walls
that shook and creaked each night the wind

swept through. A hole in the floor beside my bed
kept me informed of bad weather swelling
beneath the house. White weatherboards,
green roof, a front verandah filled in with gravel.
The outside light was like a sentry to the darkness.

# Catching a train to intimacy

The Literary world stops at Spencer Street
where ex-country people are haunted
by the fear of running into someone they might know,
the anxiety of returning home
and the relief of getting out of the city

to footy matches where you can take your car up to the fence
buy a hot dog at half-time from a woman who used to beat you at tennis
where old harvesting friends stop you in the street
to ask 'where are you working?'

then look away, distracted by the wind
as soon as you mention another job with computers.
Over the intercom, nasal accents of a conductor's voice—
'road connections to Illowa, Port Fairy, Portland.'

Like a babysitter the city releases you
into rye grass, dead eucalypts,
the people who made you leave.
The train picks up more passengers

with bad haircuts, big grins.
The conductor collects Colac tickets.
A paddock of canola
and I remember our yellow kitchen walls

mud at the gateway to the dairy,
cows bunched up after their milking
staring at paddocks darkening around them.
The train crosses the road our school bus travelled on.

These paddocks will always belong to the girl in the third seat
and queuing up under the stars for the outside toilet,
rolling dead cows onto the carry-all
hooking their legs between the bars,

the head bouncing along the gravel.
Mum measuring the years by babies
miscarriages, divorces and suicides.
Suddenly the radio—the funeral music of Beattie & Sons

stopping our talk during afternoon tea,
the announcer's voice blandly reading
'it is with regret we announce the death of …'
More tea is poured

'Who did she marry?'
'Who was her father?'
'I think she was one of …'
The train pulls in.

I step off into fresh air
the fear that memory delivers me to.
The road home is in the eye that admits you.
Behind me, the city waits like a perfect idea.

# The paddock with the big tree in it

Like an anchor rattling overboard
she turns from her mother
heaving the morning into the spin dryer
and faces the paddocks.
The smell of mud is nesting in her head.
The tractor thundering in the shed
is pulling her around.
She walks like a dancer seasoned by grief
through the cow shit on the driveway.
All sorrows are accepted
as she divides the fence wires
her pilgrim legs splayed between the paddocks
between someone buzzing the bone
and someone licking the spoon,
between the bed she warms with her sisters
and the milking a girl should never do.
She drags her rubber boots through capeweed
stands in drains to watch dirty water rise.
Like an echo she returns
to the trunk of a dead gum tree
rubbed smooth by cow's necks.
She leans into wood
electrified as prayer.

# Maternity paddock

Chopped up by staggery cows
circling for shelter

by dawn
it's a battlefield.

Three dead calves
smear the dirt

mouths open
tongues hanging out.

Overnight
half their stomachs disappeared.

In the next couple of days
their ribcages will be trodden into mud

Larry might drag a head into his kennel.

Each morning two or three calves survive
this paddock

that is close enough to light up
with a spotty from the porch.

In the pre-dawn warmth
this is the view you rely on

to discover
which cows need the birth ropes.

Two days after the birth
the calf is separated from its mother.

The dairy becomes an opera of bawling calves
distraught cows running back and forward

milk dribbling beneath them.
The calf-buyer heaves the bulls

into the darkness of his truck.
Another calf hobbles through the mud

towards her mother's teats.
In moments like these

dogs keep their distance
from staggery cows making this paddock their own.

# A paddock in his head

Clouds wedged between two Commission towers
as if wanting release
like an anger between words

unspoken, brooding, an absence
relentless as bush wind.
He carries a paddock in his head

that has been ploughed, disked and harrowed,
where the horizon is a boundary fence
holding in what he knows of this land.

He takes the paddock into the city
imagines the streets in knee-length rye grass,
a single eucalypt, over-arching sky.

Like a country footballer lost on a footy trip
he stands his ground, trusting no-one
the skies he knew as a child

torment him like TV weather maps each night.
The crowds hustle around him
as if he was a corner, an alcove

to be ignored, a place occupied by wind—
a man standing in rye grass
looking for fences and a sky to be held in.

# Tower Hill

Driving into the crater
past shelves of basalt, clinker and limestone

I wait for my aunt's stories.
She remembers a king tide claiming the paddocks

a house being lifted, then taken away by a river.
We cross a causeway to the island

and pass Mitsubishis and Pajeros looking for emus.
Every time my parents drove out to Koroit

I struggled to glimpse the lake through the trees.
I was looking for a rupture,

a tearing in the flow of my family stories.
Just as limestone rises with the pressure of gas

locals have left pubs on Friday nights
and driven over the lip

of the eastern embankment, flying
into nothingness with a grin

for two hundred feet.
My mother and her sister are discussing the weekend footy scores.

I want to hear more about the neighbour who drowned in a puddle.
'You don't want to know that.'

West of the lookout
the jagged script of Norfolk pines

smudging the horizon
and then closer, like the joy

in my aunt's stories of Ernie
breakers on Killarney beach.

Here, where light is incidental to wind
Von Guerard's painting has become a guide

for a revegetation program. Birds
have been returned, rabbits poisoned.

an Aboriginal history is allowed
and not talked about. Who owns the stories

the sloping caldera slips into?
I think of our old blue Holden rolling

back down the exit road
the handbrake failing

and of looking in fear to that view—
reedy swamps and strangling roots,

the terrible cries
we weren't allowed to hear.

# Uncles and aunties

A man remains in his car while his mother is buried.
What I know of them is unreliable, a cousin to truth.

A woman examines the cracks in her brother's new lino squares.
Shadows of my father, they come alive in stories.

There are people walking across paddocks banging saucepans.
A silver watch belonging to an uncle, the thickness of his wrist
                              matching mine.

A man buries his mother, and then two days later, his wife.
My aunts were better hand-milkers than my uncles.

A man returns from a bout in hospital to a unit in Murtoa.
At what point does the fiction begin?

At 29, a man dies on Christmas Day.
Eventually, truth becomes a matter of the last remaining voice.

Two sisters are serving in the rail canteen at Camperdown.
My father thumping the table just before the News.

A woman drives the same car for thirty years.
Some stories couldn't be told in front of children.

The apiarists were travelling south through the Wimmera to recruit workers.
After the first deaths, my father's stories became funnier.

He is a man who will work one day, sit around for the next four.
They would call in unannounced and my brother would hide in the wardrobe.

When you sat down at the table, there was always a dog darting
                                          out between your legs.
In a crowded city gallery, the country is on the walls, on their faces,
                                          in their football conversations.

A man is carried out of church on the shoulders of his sons.
Distances opening when an aunt walks in the room.

# Hayseeds

Undulating paddocks of round bales
light beating off the stubble.
Seen from above, the uniform rows
could be an installation, a comment on form
giant yellow balls dropped from the sky.
Could they be anything else but
icons of summer?—endless teenage years
when everything was being worked out,
worked at, in weeks of work except
then it was square bales, acres of them
and my first real money: picking off the baler
edges up on the back of a truck
following *The Weekly Times* stack plan
heat climbing as I listened to the talk—
who had five thousand pressed
who might buy that out-paddock at Cudgee,
while I sweated over girls
I might see at Mass on Sunday.
I discovered there was honour in work
in being seen to do something successfully,
a game I played with friends to see
who carted in the most bales.
Farmers live by their reputations
I had hayseeds in my eyes.
I knew I was missing out on parties, dates
prowling through beach caravan parks,
except none of this could account for the light
once we'd emptied the paddocks.

# A walk to the supermarket

Late Sunday quiet, shutters down
light polishing the tram tracks
a few people out walking, taking in
the sights: a charred video sign
a chemist, a change is expected

but the air won't deliver.
A woman leans out of her 4WD to spit
waits until I pass, then lets go.
No buskers outside the supermarket
just a bloke drinking at the corner bench

one block the other way a bar is jammed
any guess its life span. I walk toward
the auto-teller, thinking of dodgy country towns
a seedy four room motel beside the pub
the gaps between people filled

by a flickering screen, regulars
two beers from being narky—
'that blinkin stinkin' coot!'
Change on the bar towel, ciggies
and lighter neat as hay bales

reading each other like back roads
frosted glass keeping the world outside.
Here, Cash Converters is taking music to the street
a rap to living on a stash, like always turning
on the red arrow. A man being chased

then collared in the gutter won't make it
on a tourist brochure. Like Tintern Abbey
the Commission Flats embedded in a landscape,
burnt-out shops and peak hour gridlocks
a sort of damaged picturesque—

dribbling from a hot dog at 3am
or the view from a party above a KFC.
Every moment a surprise, as if seeing the city
the first time, except these warehouses
are haunted by parties of not knowing

who to talk to, nodding to jazzy circus acts.
Funny how office space resurrects memory
and an empty street can pulse with people
you no longer see. Like the way four farmers
in a pub can focus on the carpet for a minute,

something more than money takes me shopping.
A lemming drawn to the familiar
I stuff plastic bags in the supermarket recycle bin.
Over the P.A, Service 100 has the fruit stackers
leaping the check-outs, racing up to the car park,

before calm descends—u.v lights, 80s hits.
Watching what other people buy
I sign for what I cannot afford, gaining
a petrol discount, more bags than I can carry
and the life I've been meaning to live.

# Teenage riot

*After Sonic Youth*

The lurid colours of the in-flight map
become an instant geography lesson.
I'm attempting to travel light

because it's heroic to walk into Asia
with a towel and toothbrush.
Why is the act of leaving so straightforward?

A ticket, a plane and a trolley load of alcohol
is wheeled toward you.
What is it that keeps us anchored to land?

Is it enough to lose yourself in the drone
of a light plane, to imagine the life you are not living
in the white lie of a jet in a cobalt blue sky?

Living on an island, the desire to leave
pushes many to the edge—I too
stood in the circles at football club barrels

listening to and watching men list
under the pressure to drink, guffaw
become the men others had imagined.

My stories, always slightly off-key
as I faltered with punch lines
the way a teenager punches for communication.

I grew up steeped in distances
where men chased sons with stock whips
and the dust from a tractor two miles away

reminded me why men kept themselves busy
when the paddocks are full of stillness and light.
The plane begins to taxi, a rush of panic mixes

with the opening chords of *Teenage Riot*.
What I am leaving will never return
but haunts me the way a cow sniffs

at the bones of a carcass, knowing
memory will bring me back to earth
and yet, like the guitars, sets me free.

# A breather

While my brother milks
I return to mist drifting up the fence posts,
the night's sheet slowly evaporating
giving in to day—already a process of action:

cows backing off the platform
making their way up the track,
the stumps of their tales flicking at flies
they regard me with surprise.

Three heifers bolt past the day's paddock
their routine has been damaged
eventually they will find their way back
as I have

habitually heading for the river
its overlaying branches, and this morning
light dispersing shadows, loosening memories
arguments

running like fissures
through how it feels to walk the paddocks—
found in things, images that linger for days
like the way moss hangs

in a water trough
and the semi-circles of scalloped mud
surrounding it.
Wind picks up

and my skin begins to prickle
at the bank of ferns
where my father almost stood on a snake
trying to chase a cow back across the swollen river.

Imitating the voice of its newborn calf
I baaed at the mother whose ears
pricked up as she stumbled around tussocks
and my father's swearing.

Somehow the connection held
and the cow swam back to the calf
sniffed her, and like an aged couple
they hobbled off as if they had never been apart.

Two ducks glide down
braking over river shadows, their feet
pushing forward against air, against time
like a memory asserting itself, found

flung out. Sounds carry for miles
a crow can dominate sixty acres—
and closer, the incessant buzzing of flies
builds like a welter around my temples,

'enough to send you round the twist'
until wind rushes through the river flats
scooping leaves, bending rye grass, a thistle
shivers.

Fenced off for a breather
the paddock has been allowed to get away.
An electrified tape strung across the track
shapes routine. Cows follow their noses.

Their tracks no more than a foot wide
give direction like a parent's voice
around the boundary line at the footy
they are also enough to stumble through,

even flat terrain has its ruts
potholes that become a part of you
like the defiant stance of a cow
eyeing me off, wondering

never quite trusting. Something uneasy
as a farmer's silence at the sale yards
passes between us. It seems enough to know
what my brother doesn't need to explain.

# Back roads, local roads

canola's chemical yellow rises above the fence line
Black Polls laze around a dam, ibis and egrets gliding overhead
wattle, casuarina, eucalypt, cypress, radiata

where the bitumen gives way to gravel
taking you deeper into shadows, ditches
tinder undergrowth of a bush block

a passing glance to a dry weather only track—
a mystery like the roads memories rise from
conversations you have to have

with the road the school bus went on
where three footballers were killed on motor bikes
how one road can define an attitude

to land, scandals dividing neighbours
local roads become stages where jealousies,
differences are played out—to wave or not to wave

look aways after church, fence lines cut
and repaired around a kitchen table, dust
catching in the throat the windows wound up

stories seeping through—the schools you went to
women defined by maiden names, back roads
connecting cousins, that family who lets their chooks in the house

light through a plantation's façade
the suspension rising and falling with each random thought
the speedo steady as fear of a family death

abandoned stockyards, shearing sheds, a colonial farmhouse
real estate on the rise leaving a flock of pelicans behind
where driving 20ks for a can of paint becomes a mission

a diversion from the tail-gating highway stare
those times after shopping in Warrnambool,
my brothers and sisters spilling out of the car at the factory

Mum's sighing gaze as Dad stirs the mechanics—
'You Labor shits!' A bag of oats weighing us down
on the slow drive back through dairy country

weatherboards and poplar driveways, red flags for the calf buyers
on strips of bitumen snaking down to Brucknell Creek,
a canopy of gums overhead, bark peeling in sluggish heat

remnants of bush stranded in a paddock of turnips
a Hereford's fur caught on a barbed wire fence
amongst roadside ferns, fallen branches, beer cans

chip packets, bull ants and places where somebody had a leak
chasing the myth of the back road short cut
farmers see more than they bargain for

teenagers leave signature burn outs
and shooters nurse a 'traveller' to give each other a hard time
knowing that the road that leads to Laang is a prick of a road in winter

through dry stone dairy country, houses set off the road
houses where the rosary was intoned and The Missions
brought families into a kitchen; embarrassed, polite, reverting

to the familiar—kneeling on lino to pray,
whose sons worked in quarries, fought on Friday nights
daughters either married early or left in a hurry

like the Warramyea Road dropping down into a gully
or the brief onset of cool from a pine plantation around Tank Hill
a reservoir I shied away from, squashed against the back seat window

I retreated into myself, the memory of playing kick to kick in a paddock
with a bull sniffing at my calves, my cousins breaking up
the road becomes an avenue of associations circling

like a sparrowhawk zeroing in to a patch of grass
the drives Dad took us on—the tip, the farms he worked
until geography becomes a matter of memory

Saturday mornings with the smell of polished footy boots
on the patched road to Woorndoo
gravel edges unreliable as the images I cling to

back roads enclosing us like growth rings on a tree

it is where grass grows up to the bitumen
that determines your longing as if being closer
to roadside weeds will allow your desires release

to dream between saplings, run your fingers
along the curves of the week's conversations
wondering did they truly describe you: a smile

a raised eyebrow, what you accepted
the absence of desire unsettling like the bump
the road makes over a level crossing

the sky released from barriers holds you to the road
hooking around a creek bed, a sudden kiss of gravel beneath the tyres
a single lane bridge and two horses either side of the road pining

'loneliness is what's killing Australia' but I am driving to stay alive
pulling over into soft edges to let a milk tanker pass
I remember the dream of this section of road

where bulls were charging people who had stopped to rest
beside a row of pine trees in failing light
now they've severed the trees exposing the dream

I've heard that horses will avoid places where the light shivers
dream places with high magnetic readings like crucifixes
tied to white posts or piles of rocks stacked in paddocks—

ramshackle cairns pulling you in, interrupting
the sweeping stare the road suddenly widens
as if direction is simply a matter of revelation

why travel the highway when you can take back roads
through paddocks and towns where the General Store and churches
closed long ago and the remnants of butter factories and walk-through dairies

crumble beside the road like conversations let go,
lives memorialized by signs—*Wild Dogs Keep Out*
local knowledge, local wars, dips and ridges reflecting a landscape

of bitten attitudes towards difference—a woman speaks out
farmers return to their beers, cow shit on the bitumen
rye grass covering the fence line the familiarity of trips

to the milk bar, nursery, out-paddock, gravel roads owning your thoughts
of speeding between sheoaks, their weeping shelter brushing your vision
as you drive out of memory, out of necessity, local roads that get you there

# A TIGHT CIRCLE

# Woman wearing a hairnet

Hooded eyes, eyelashes thinning, she tailgates a semi
keeping up with him in case she breaks down.
The truckie has her measure in his rear-view mirror—
an old Falcon tracking the loneliness between Horsham and Koroit.
Wide verges, scoria tracks radiating back to chimneyed farmhouses
the country she passes through steadies her like a needle:
years of croquet, bowls and a Depression habit of not spending.
She sighs for the woman on the truck's mud flaps
and the boyfriends she could never marry.
Her hands swim around the steering wheel
as a diminishing list of names falls from her lips.
A carrier of stories, the lowdown on brothers and sisters
she pushes the semi along chipped bitumen
towards her younger brother's 70th. From a distance
it is difficult to see what is holding this freighted load,
as if one woman's memories could keep a truckie honest,
an unlikely duo marrying the district.
She heels the accelerator
and with a flick of the wrist he waves her on.

# Talking to auntie

Something is on your back doorstep
and you don't realise how big it is.

With her cataracts removed
her grey slacks have turned blue

and her stories become slanted
when my mother walks in the room.

Plunger Pat, Shine Ryan, Birregurra Bill.
She slips into a church that smells of onions

a man who dined with his mother
instead of a wife each night.

Like hot tea filled to the brim
I've inherited a world

that doesn't guarantee the present.
In a kitchen bathed with light

she offers me dry biscuits
another blind auntie smiling beneath cataracts.

'I feel like I'm cutting my throat
if I don't eat some potatoes each day.'

I ask for stories and she gives me facts
so strange, they must be fiction.

Everything she owns is moored to memory
passed around to the music of a footy commentary.

'Do you want another cup of tea?
No, well you're not a tea drinker then.'

I was thirteen when she gave me a cigar
behind the hummocks at Killarney beach.

Her skin is wrinkled
as a farm in Tyrendarra

his enlistment at lunch
a soldier settlement in Tarrone

a brick veneer in Koroit.
Like entries in a farmer's diary

her stories shadow Aboriginal history.
She lives between the friends who have died

and cards each fortnight. Making do
collapsing after two beers on a hot afternoon.

# A tight circle

At my uncle's grave the undertakers
ask us to come in closer, form a tight circle.
A big ask, for a family made straggly by grief.
Some need distance from the hole.
A stranger wearing an Essendon beanie
stands close. Who does he belong to?

The priest has a glint in his eye.
He is on home turf, was raised
a paddock away. His father,
buried nearby, grew up picking spuds.
My uncle drove trucks for a living
cut down bush for firewood,
but was too weak for a new pacemaker.
Only two days ago
he was gasping for breath in a hospital ward
his body shelled, one eye quivering in the light.

The undertakers, former farmers
who most people know and are beginning to trust
give instructions to my cousins
on how best to lower my uncle into the darkness.
Nose-first, they jockey him under the concrete lip
then slowly relinquish their grip
on the lowering straps. We mutter
through the Lord's Prayer
as highway traffic streams past.
My father and his sisters step carefully
over loose clods of dirt.
The beanie rests on the coffin.
Burying has aged my father
softened his handshake.

He wakes in the night to exercise his new replacement knee.
Each afternoon he leans against the front fence
with his crutches talking to anybody who'll stop—
he has to know what's going on
and when he'll be allowed to drive out to the farm
to see the cows
bunched up in the yard
forming a tight circle.

# Factory boys

White overalls, rubber boots and a hairnet
a red surname sewn into the chest pocket,
I was ready. To sacrifice sunlight
for the punishing noise of steel clanging on steel
revolving guillotine blades carving lengths of cheese,
the pressure on my feet
from eight hours of standing beside a conveyor belt
checking steel containers clasping blocks of cheddar
shunting past like minutes, each one counted,
then hands whirling over steel in the washroom
overalls soaked and inventing jokes with the Yank
from Detroit who hates cheese, work and Aussies,
both of us shouting above the clamour
as if opinions ever mattered when the stainless steel
was piling up around us.

A week later, the shifts have become ingrained
jobs so familiar I finish them in my sleep—
checking valves, testing rennet, twisting
stainless steel taps to switch milk between vats.
For the permanents, extended tea breaks are ignored.
The supervisors take walks between 3 and 4am.
The seasonal casuals—hungover, love bites on the neck
wheel 44 gallon drums of cheese offcuts
under the crusher. We are paid above the award.

One night after two weeks on late shift
I fell asleep, clipped a white post, did a 180
on the crest of a hill, shimmied up an embankment
slammed into bluestone rocks, headlights
shining into my sister-in-law's bedroom.
Next week in the tearoom it barely rated a mention.

We lived for the buzz of our pay slip
dragging each other off as we left the car park,
racing the train to the road crossing
that one of us didn't make. Our faces
turning pasty as the hunks of cheese
we kicked around the concrete floor.

# Back streets

not the zoned stares of tollways, freeway art and
        variable speed limits
not the avenues of discount warehouses, superstores
        and car yards
but the back street short cuts between suburbs

where children kick footballs between approaching cars
and decorate the road with hop-scotch squares on
        Sunday afternoons
where workers' cottages are made over by new
        generations

stringing prayer flags across verandahs, smoking on
        front doorsteps
mesmerised by pigeons on antennas, neighbours
        fighting for car spaces
where the idea of home becomes graffiti on a
        corrugated iron wall

the Gipps Street dogleg that takes you past Nike and
        the Salvos
into the clutter of Richmond, the high rises, tyres
        slipping on the tram tracks

in the eternal quest to avoid Punt Road traffic—a daily purgatory
        your fantasies idling through a gridlock
the thrum of tyres on bluestone cobbles
or the scrape of a number plate in the gutter

as you nose-dive into an alley between backyards
searching for an escape from one-way streets that take you closer
to junk mail in letter boxes,

an empty stubbie outside the stairwell to a block of flats
the suburban street not needing to flood
or be pummelled by a road train to be memorable—

a distinctive house on a corner, a moment's drift at the lights
the pilgrimage of men to the shop for the Sunday papers
will keep returning years later

# Choppers

Skin and bone cows
cast out from the herd

lame, slack-bellied and undershot
they get head-butted into gateposts

and put in a paddock of thistles
to raise abandoned calves.

Between April and May
the chopper season begins.

Herds are cleaned up
any mongrel not pulling her weight

is sent up the road.
For two hundred bucks

they might be worth the gamble
to young farmers hungry for a quick grand

but who wants a barren cow
even the bulls have lost interest in.

You know what a chopper is worth
by the way she carries her head,

how she walks into the sale ring.
If nobody raises a finger

she is knocked down
to the abs and knackery buyers,

always in the bidding.

# On chook time

The headless chicken spiralling away
from my father's hands, scattering blood
in a frenzied arc I had not seen before.

Our chooks straddle my hold on the past
Isa Browns instead of Leghorns, four eggs
warming the kitchen table talk each day.

They lead me into darkened corners
under shelves, into the cobwebbed woodheap.
Fossicking under birch trees

they dig as they please, while my mother's voice
catches me—'chop some wood, feed the chooks
Arr? Can't hear you?' The daily banter I renew

with my daughters, their words scraping
beneath the surface while the chooks
scatter pea straw, flick back powdery dirt.

They scratch in packs
yet my daughters' playtimes flex and contract
swinging between inside and outside

together, apart, together, apart
pulling off dolls' heads, mixing mud pies,
fairy dancing. The chooks have mown

the perimeter of the chicken wire enclosure.
Stretching their necks through the fence
to peck at fresh grass. If any thing

I've learnt to look for, not necessarily listen to
the past flashing through each day. A southerly
busts through. The garage door lifts and clangs.

The chooks sprint in a fixed line across the lawn:
heads flattened, wings raised, chirruping all the way
reminding me of the chooks on Ash Wednesday

zig-zagging along the fence's edge, fear
in the way I ran from their eyes.
My brothers and sisters used to roost on the rails

each of us screeching, flapping elbows in failing light
or the flailing lights of memory, off-cue.
The chooks lay where I least expect them to.

My younger daughter repeats each new word
I give to her; quietly storing them as jewels, as toys.
Chooks live by habits of the mind. My footfalls

to the paper down the driveway get them talking.
Each day is a result of their scratching.
It is the past getting into my heart.

# TRAVELLING THROUGH THE FAMILY

# Blister country

The anger of living in the country
remains with you, becomes a hard stare
across a playground, a bar, a supermarket checkout.
Here, we look after our own.
of talking business with men, problems with women.
Of being bashed in pub toilets
of being jeered at for wearing black
of fleeing each weekend, the town closing for the footy.
Saturday night, four men lined up at a urinal,
nobody speaks.

Stunted trees, lemon-tinged rye grass.
lava blisters formed by pressure from below.
A moonscape of low-lying paddocks
the country nobody inhabits.
A wild place, I'll nurture, carry to the grave.
There's nothing flash in hummocks of rock,
Old Crusher Road snaking through Harman's Valley,
and what became of the lava flow.

Here, wind is another language to rub against
buffeting faces, breaking capillaries across cheeks.
Where fence lines hum off-key,
a place so strange and compelling
a boy rides a motorbike down the paddock to shoot himself.
The tension between rains prises the dirt apart,
crickets scurry.
Some kind of friction rises from within.

# A dark place

Utes prowl the flatlands, high beaming
piles of trees ready for burn-off.
Our spotties sweep ahead reclaiming the night
the darkness shadowed by wind.

We head into a paddock where the roos congregate
or so the stories suggest. We drink,
twitch at the glow of eyes scurrying away from the sights
tense at a heavier shadow bounding away
to the right. A 30/30 is loaded.
The driver flattens it
until we are surfing branches and rocks,
steadying our stubbies as the mob dives to the left.
One falls and we pull up.
Someone walks over to a joey, blasts it.
I empty my .270 into a big Grey, yet he remains there
shaking his head, as if asking 'what are you doing?'
With a guttural moan, he falls.
The pelt still warm, the vacant eyes.
I'm earning my keep with the stories that flow
long into the night. There is a quota
that must be observed, acknowledged
like peppering a red gum with a machine gun,
or watching white posts merge
doing the ton. Somebody hands me a beer
and the tension between us becomes folklore,
a place from where nicknames are created.
There's another mob caught out near a boundary fence.
Our spotties frame them leaping head-first
into the wire mesh, again and again.

# Abattoir sonnet

Night cries of cattle from the sale yards.
Industrial, scrubby land between railway and paddock
where semi-trailers rattle and shudder before roundabouts,
where the smell of slaughterhouses is carried
east, away from the plaintive call of vealers.
Nearby in a caravan park people cluster around TVs
volume cranked up, forensic dramas competing
with the unmistakable bellow of a bull.

I clean my teeth in the amenities block
thinking of the smell of dead cow on my father's clothes
when he came home from the knackery.
How dead animals stayed in the car for days
like a memory in need of air, a reminder
tomorrow some cow will receive a bolt in the head.

# The killing work

The Hereford steer from wild country that charged our Valiant as we tried to shift it into a fresh paddock. Herd leader, cantankerous, fearless; a beast we couldn't trust. Dents in the quarter panels, tongue swipes on the bumper. We reverse away from the lowered horns, pushed deeper into the paddock. My father swearing, wrenching the steering wheel left, right, wheels skidding over cape weed. My brother and I in the back seat look away from what we know is not quite right. Not a time to speak with a beast on the loose, tearing through a barbed wire fence, flipping over, an apparent heart attack. We stare at the frothing mouth. My father silenced. The Hereford steer from wild country left on the track for the knackery truck.

>scrubbed concrete floors
>latex gloves, Muslim slaughtermen
>rows of carcasses slide towards you

Returning from away, I ask about our pet cow Beefy—a cross-bred black dairy cow. The only cow we could hug, nuzzle, who would amble up to us, raise her head to sniff, rub against us. Not a productive milker, the type of cow who recognizes her own presence, unafraid of dogs, almost personable. 'You're eating her,' came the reply. Cut down, packed into plastic bags, steaks and ribs piled high in the Deep Freeze. A family has to eat. We ate steaks for breakfast, dinner and tea yet rarely butchered our own. Deaths in the paddock were acceptable, regrettable, something to rise from while talking around the red Laminex table, those heifers that need to be ear-tagged.

# Summer grasses

Summer grasses have swallowed the Fargo ute.
Its crumpled chassis barely visible
beneath the seed-heads, their inflorescence
concealing like memory, perennial rye grass
rising through the windscreen, stems
wavering against gaping headlights.
A dislodged bumper-bar rests like a broken arm.
A fallen tree only seems to push the ute
further into the ground. Nature conspiring
slow burial, a giving-in to earth.
More of a paddock bomb than a working ute
an uncle's gift we drove in figure-eights
until its muffler dropped off, a piston shot through
to jokes and one liners—it was a carnival ride
belting through ditches in the Fargo ute.
Now summer grasses let go their seeds
across its roof. Exhausted of use
it rests like a venerable icon
to the rusting machinery farmers don't have the heart
to remove. Memory is sacred.
Summer grasses can have the Fargo ute.

# Vacant blocks

Infested with dock weed, thistles, rocks and concrete,
pepper trees, woolly acacias, pallets, chicken wire and clay.
The fenceless territory between our thoughts
breathing places for a rural town
waiting to be owned, returned to, ignored.
Empty, unused, oh so pretty, an eyesore.
The vacant block over the fence
offering distance from your mortgage.
These shapes between houses, corner blocks
nobody wants, home to wandery teenagers,
stubbies turfed from passing cars.
The hinterland between kerb and paddock
where families are yet to take hold,
dreaming spaces where the sky gets in
where somebody parks a caravan on under-utilised land,
where a Portaloo and a slab of concrete
spells community progress. On Sundays
dark BMWs trawl the gravel streets
looking for infrastructure.

# Cowshit

Smell of country air, of cow shit in the grass
in the dairy, on farmer's arms, on jeans, shirts
leather aprons, cowshit dripping off the rails
squeegeed down drains, piped into paddocks.
One farmer's waste becomes a supermarket essential.
It's cowshit economics. The word that dare not
be admitted determines class, roughness, is
the perfume in a dairy farmer's bedroom.
The shit stains on my forearm from rolled-up sleeves
have remained a tattoo of the smell that greets me
each time I return, step out of the car into long grass
checking for a soft explosion beneath my feet.
A boot full of cowshit and I am back plunging through
calf-deep mud outside the dairy
cowshit oozing down to my socks
my rubber boots weighted by cowshit conditions.

The smell that carries flies
a darkness that lives beneath fingernails.
Farmers study their cows through cowshit—
a runny jet-stream when a cow is steamy and bullin',
dried clumps when her milk is off.
Never a good idea to light a match when a tail is being lifted.
Its uses are sacred. In Varanasi, cow dung is collected
left to dry beside washed saris stretched along the ghats.
In Panmure, little green haloes are spread across Spring paddocks.
Cows on the road always leave a Hansel and Gretel trial
a splattering that reflects the meditative sway of their walk.
Dogs avoid it. A spray of cowshit on an SUV lends credibility.
A cowshit-flecked face suggests battle
the stain sheep farmers avoid.
Dairy farming is the lowest of the low.
The air that colours skin, seeps into cuts and wrinkles.
I smell my hands and I smell a district.

# Man on the gate

Oilskin keeping out the cold
the muscles in his legs wearing down
through the under 12s, netball, under 14s,
under 18s, reserves and finally seniors around two.
A job we all expect somebody to do.
A man who complements the scene
of cars nosed up to the boundary fence,
kids walking around with a piece of cardboard
displaying the winning raffle ticket.
Panicked voices rifling through the air—
'kick it Moorey.' The crowd by the clubrooms
groaning like an ancient ship—red faces, stubbie holders,
Club jackets sponsored by local businesses,
a gathering necessary as a pie from the canteen.
Certain women cheerfully hand over Cherry Ripes,
polystyrene cups with scalding tea. Each person
connected through marriage, kinder, school
or just plain proximity. Generations of neighbours
realizing their duty, lives flowing through moments
of a job—somebody has to blow the siren,
somebody has to cut up oranges into quarters,
somebody has to collect the footy after it sails
over Monk's barbed wire fence,
somebody has to sit in a car with kids climbing over seats.
It is a scene that swells through the afternoon
like the feet of the man on the gate
shifting his weight on the gravel,
puffy, arthritic fingers fumbling
with the texture of crisp notes.
A small town's investment in belief.
A community finding something to do.
Each year, he says, will be the last.

# Travelling through the family

She floats between rooms
on the waves of talkback radio.
Nursing their opinions, frustrations,
warmth of a footy analysis.
She carries the radio the way
she used to carry a child—one arm
always free, sustained, in rhythm to days
traced by a worn carpet path,
a clock radio muttering in a darkened bedroom.

After ten births and six different addresses
she has become a Tai Chi devotee.
She has given me my facial expressions
the indignant rising tone of an earnest voice,
the bond we sense by the need
to stand beside each other in a room.
She asks will I be home for tea, knowing
the repetition of roast chicken is enough.
I imagine her special trip to the supermarket
knowing this is just something parents do.

                    In the sunroom
on an antique table, place mats of Sydney
beneath our plates of boiled pumpkin, chicken and gravy.
A cup of tea following each meal confirms
the world will not end, despite
the sun marks on her face that scare me,
my fears that she could be slipping
further into footy commentaries.
Dutifully, we argue about politics and Aborigines.
She washes, I wipe, and tells me the songs
she wants played at her funeral.

I consider the songs she sang on the radio as a four-year old.
The voice I didn't hear, passed down to me,
a heartbeat travelling through the family.

# Mother and daughter

A photo of her from the brown suitcase—
a fourteen-year-old in pigtails, pleated tunic
Saturday morning optimism.
Her primly dressed mother beside her
setting the pace. Their lives held
by the mother's formal gaze, a wariness
owing to the black and white era.
One of the few creased photos of my mother
before her office job, before marriage.
She has the innocent air of being in life;
an ordinary moment developing, unaware
that much later she would stagger
from a farmhouse to a neighbour's dairy
about to give birth and wanting a lift.
Perhaps the photo lacks the truth
of men throwing chooks through the windows
of the Crossley Hall dances, or the lifts
my father gave her to the Pictures
with her mother, up front, sitting in between them.
What can be trusted—the intent of her eyes
the future I throw back at her,
a mother and daughter stepping out
of a busy country street,
going somewhere without being able to arrive.

# Equilibrium

This is where we are at our most equal
sitting across from each other at a Laminex table.
Children in bed, released from work
and the dilemnas we magnify,
(those dark drives back to the verandah light).
We come back to conversations left
hanging in the day. The camper van's
fan heater switches itself off after cooking up.
Its teasing heat seems enough as the bags of clothes
we have to move to sit down.
Easy nights of camping are rare and valued
as the thumping of waves outside.
Anybody can sink into a Wilderness chair
with a stubbie and take in the view—
this is where our lives return to.
Unpolished moments of you writing
the sound of a page being turned,
a memory surfacing, we step back
into the country we've made.
So much is afforded between these canvas walls
some lost moment we've learnt to dwell in,
accept the way hard weather throws people together.
The fan heater settles into another cycle
yet as the darkness sidles through the banksias
the van shudders with the aftershocks. Earlier on,
there were stars I tracked on my last trip
to the dunny, equations of light I could
barely believe in. Hunted by what I heard
of the night, I followed the torch light back
to the glow of our van, sighing for
equilibrium.

# True confessions

The red velvet curtain parting
the miniature wooden door sliding back
a man's face able to be smelt.

'Bless me father for I have sinned.'
My sins are lying, being rude to a sister,
eyeing off women in Mass.

'Is there anything else?'
Pure and impure thoughts
desires I can't talk about.

A monotone absolution, my mood
lightening as I race through
The Act of Contrition.

Relieved, almost giddy to be free
I join locals kneeling before candles on the altar,
the women who stay longer.

I want to be contrite—
it appears to be the done thing.
My sins have been heard

a part of me has been released—
absurd! My sins were made up
rehashed, reheated, pre-loved.

Like others, lying in the confessional
became a duty—inventing sins to keep the peace,
to assuage the guilt that never leaves.

The first of many contradictory Catholic beliefs.
The distance in the man's voice
rattling through cool absolving words.

Were the priests cheated too, as I was?
Or did they come to trust a congregation
by the stories told in confession?

# Tour of duty

St Brendan's, where I learnt to hold a plate
beneath the tongues of locals. Robed
in surplice and cassock, eyeing off the congregation,
I saw what ritual and prayer does to faces,
how a district organizes itself into rows, favoured pews.
The priests had little doubt who they were talking to.
The essence of ritual is returning.
The farmers and their families
were religious as their milking.
The altar where I learnt to ring a bell, balance
the cruets. Christ's feet were always bleeding
as babies crying were carried outside,
away from the smokers who would politely enter
at the Consecration, then leave after Communion,
roll cigarettes and lean against weatherboards.
What happened outside Mass affected a community—
men clustering into conversations
girls comparing weekends or rushing
to wait in cars for fathers, while the priest
smiled into farmers' confidences.
Everybody suddenly became polite:
mothers fussing, laughing at his jokes.
a three-metre concrete square attained the life of a party:
the quiet brooders, the listeners, the elevators,
the show-offs, the weekly pious.
Within an hour we were all leaving
for World of Sport and The Sunday Press.

# Philip Hodgins

I walk toward a paddock bordered by cypress trees.
Philip Hodgins is on a tractor harrowing 40 acres.
I can't see his face but I know it is him
methodically going about his business,
navigating the terrain, driving into a diminishing
square, like the farmer in *Dispossessed* mowing lucerne,
driving rabbits and snakes into a disappearing centre.
Except here, windrows of dirt pile up in lines
behind the tractor, a symmetry of harrowed soil,
not unlike a Buddhist mandala, rippling out toward
the boundary fence in waves one to two feet high.
He gives the tractor some throttle. The windrows of dirt
are stopping me from entering the paddock.
I want to ask him about his lines
yet sense that I will never get close to him.
He seems to be on a mission to work the paddock
to its own manic rhythm. I measure my distance,
windrows of dirt brush against me.

In another dream he is holding a shotgun at me
pointing it between my eyes. He is looking down the barrel.
He seems tired, resigned yet determined.
This is about the time I am writing my thesis
on his poetry. His rhythmic lines intersecting in my head,
His untimely death, direct nature of his address—
'There's nothing in these dying days'
consumes me and I live in two worlds,
grappling for an argument like a rock-climber
who has lost his footing, arms and legs flailing
for a ledge. He is looking down the barrel at me—
'Now it is up to you, to do this work'
which confounds me. I am not up to

such direct statement. One of those moments
in a dream where I feel myself sweat,
wake soon after. A dream to burden the day—
his words, that stare down the barrel.

# Late summer light

Driving with a half-open window
night air rushing in. A hint of dry
paddocks, salt, shadows of pine and cypress
rolling past, moving into dream light
of fence silhouettes. The 5am breaking light
when the waking fears subside, except now
the dark is reversed by a suggestion of moonlight,
backlit paddocks, the road rising out of a gully.
Everything that has been piling up has been released.
What this late summer night promises
some call freedom—last gasp of sultry heat,
couples on balconies in the new estates,
footy returning in the coming weeks.
There are flashes in the sky that could be stars
yet I've learnt to dream by the wing lights
of descending planes, mesmerized by their paths
through cloud. Unburdened of air, grounded
by deadlines, I'm learning to fly.

## *from* Driving sonnets

iv

A strip of single lane bitumen
cutting a line through paddocks is where I'm happiest.
No car, billboards or evidence of road safety.
Just ruins of farm houses or the space
where a house was between clumps of trees.
Driving through back country is driving into possibility,
cogitation, a ruminant type of thinking. Chewing things over
without the need to make a decision, pondering
old dairies, shadowy outline of Mt Elephant on the horizon.
Thrum of tyres on the bitumen, what gravel can do to the heart.
The spaces between my life and the road I'm holding onto.
The gaps in our conversations where a thought is let go,
grappled with. Ideas we circle for days.
Driving through memory is doing a 180 down a back country lane.

## V

My mother never mastered the clutch.
She'd rev the engine, keep her foot on the pedal.
while trying to the shunt the HR into gear.
All of us heaving forward as the school bus pulled away.
Each gear shift was a mind change, an exertion of will,
like five loads of washing, something she just had to do.
A line of cars behind us, sun in their eyes,
mother's red face, biting her lip, refusing to swear.
We endured, we looked down until her old confidence
returned. She coaxed the lever up, away from her
and up again. From first to second, always a difficult gesture—
too much force and the linkages jammed. I'd like to believe
with one gentle upward lift we were gliding—
stories of school, questions of dinner, the prospect of milking.

# SMALL TOWN SOUNDTRACK

# Outsider pastoral

Three regulars laugh at their own jokes
sip beers without getting their lips wet.
Hunched shoulders, flannelettes
two could be mountain men—
quiet, loyal, large, who probably
begin each day with a joint
work at the abattoir, or swivelling
the Stop/Go sign, whatever they can get.
The small woman between them
has a face stretched by experience.
She knows where the good deer are,
slags off city hunters with their high-powered rifles
'wouldn't have a clue how to butcher a beast.'
She drinks J.D. The two nod, agree.
On the wall, a poster lists
15 ways a beer is better than a woman.

Mostly, they ignore me, are used to
tourists, can keep an eye on me
while watching the Trots, shelves of spirits.
Too neat, too quiet, probably votes Green.
I'm just an outsider nursing his beer
who reeks of places anywhere but here.
When I worked in London pubs, there were men
you could set your watch to by the time
they arrived, emptied two pints, turned
with their briefcase for the Tube.
Men who had no need for conversation—
the day was in their heads. All that they had
they would give a good talking to,
eyeing off their reflections in mirrors
and brass railings, smoking John Player
when smoking was still allowed.

The woman behind the bar refills my pot
leans on the taps, chats to the mountain men.
The grins are quick and ready.
The small woman's voice rises
before they disappear to the beer garden.
The unease of remaining begins.
One more pot and the glances will extend
into questions.
'Where are you from? What are you doing?'
Growing up in the country, I learned
there is a line running like a fuse
between here and away,
between the jokes accepted
and the contentions that hold sway.
Is it better to drink with the locals
or rest your foot on the rail bristling
with accusations?
Where is the man who stuck up the poster?
The trio returns, eyes glazed, smiling.

# To do list

*In memory of Leo Seemanpillai.*

The rush to make drama class—
shoes, teeth, notebook, brushing
my daughter's hair. Anybody would think
a war had started. Still, we make it
out the door, collect her friend, enter
Saturday morning traffic. Hopeful day.
I tick off jobs from my floating to do list.
It keeps me anchored to the here and now
a mental sheet designed to stop me from drifting
through the day hopelessly unencumbered.
At the Highton Circulator,
a roundabout large as a supermarket,
an L-plater nervously edges forward.
He waits, falters, misses the gaps. I shake my head,
pound the steering wheel. SUVs and Magnas
cruise towards us before arcing away
like a show ride that promises danger
within safety rails. He makes a run for it.
Hot on his heels, pedal to the metal,
I turn to glare at drivers who have to slow for me.
My daughter and her friend rehearse lines
for an upcoming concert. Horses in a paddock
have them squealing. We pass the tents
of a Farmer's Market. Cars drop down
Shannon Avenue towards us like chicks
falling into a chute. The jobs I have to do.
I turn right into West Fyans Street
flashing blue light, police ribbons stretched
between shrubs. A policeman stands with a specimen bag,
another chats to a man on the footpath.
The girls stare. Stalled traffic.
We wait, roll forward, wait, are released

to continue staring at the ribbons,
the concrete driveway to a block of flats
that have always been there—
ugly, functional as a bad decision.
A place to live, a place to watch telly in.
We make the class, just, and I am free
to return to my list, the record of my days
I adhere to like a remora to a whale.
The radio tells me of the man
who took a container of petrol
poured it over himself and struck a match,
a man who gave his body to flames
rather than be returned to a country of torture.
His death on a patch of concrete in West Fyans Street
as I was taking my daughter to drama.
Some days I just throw the list away.

# Grounded angels

There are no angels here
and those that exist
are grounded and persistent.

Each day, a woman walks the path
to her front gate, pauses
only to slowly turn

back to the screen door
the kids, drinking husband,
the man she nursed

after the cigarettes got in.
Some kind of justice she lived
the way two loaded supermarket bags

balance a woman walking uphill.
Angels who do the clutter work
trafficking faith in God's absence.

In one week, a man buries his mother
two days after, his wife.
An aneurism, she crashed

the car about lunchtime.
Later, when the man's father
was buried, his ten-year-old son

stood in a lounge room
taking in the cousins, the silences
as if the person we had been thinking of

had quietly left the room.
Out of politeness, the boy grinned
as if it was a trick he could call upon.

# Dairy farmers at the beach

My parents were never swimmers.
They kept to their own tide, too busy
to sunbake, they wore what was needed—
floral dresses, kitchen skin, yakka pants
held up by a loose belt, blue singlet tan.

They stand on the beach, arms folded
eyeing off the water as if watching the land
for signs of history. Together they stoop
and sway, swinging their hands
at the waves, laughing, stepping back
from the wash.

For they are inland people
the beach is a type of joke not to be taken
as seriously as a basket of washing,
shifting the dry cows, or getting ready for Mass.
They rarely go in above their knees
and lay their bath towels in a place
where they can have a pitch to others.

We always had to leave Peterborough
by 3:30. While others played cricket, snoozed
or body surfed, I learned about duty
being in the dairy twice a day,
the heat of four children in the back seat
sand between our thighs, sunburn and camel bites.

Heading back through Nirranda, Nullawarre
and Naringal—cricket towns with a hall,
and a sense of the beach being once removed,
I looked out the window at other cows

plodding toward their herringbones and knew
what I was in for, what I couldn't escape—
my parents' ghostly shins flicking off water,
of never going in too deep, grounded
by what they wore to the beach.

# Sign of peace

When my uncle was dying
my father drove three hours
along chipped country roads to see him.
All my uncle wanted to do
was grunt and shake my father's hand.
Most of his life, my uncle had lived alone,
had never really had the need to shake hands
unlike my father who has had six sons
thrusting their right hand at him for seventy years.

Reclusive, unmarried, exiled to Murtoa,
the uncle who lived as an unanswered question
until I saw his photo on the funeral service pamphlet.
He might have been happy with the cigarettes,
the friend down to take care of the belongings
after the funeral. Perhaps other people too,
reach a point when they are ready to shake hands,
to touch another person's skin
like the sign of peace before Communion,
when people turn to shake hands
with strangers, those nearest, brothers.

# Small town pastoral

The uncle thumping the nephew in the guts.
The footballer dancing topless on the bar.
I wake to a sugar gum in a paddock of ferns
towering cypress trees collapsing along Vickers' Road
the diamond blaze of summer light everywhere.

My father rarely talks of what he does in there.
He gives us silences, the presence of killing in the air.

Shovelling bones and intestines onto a conveyor belt
skinning a dead horse or cow one minute
wiping maggots off his jeans,
tucking into a meat pie the next.

Sometimes the smell of a chopper
my brother and I let out in the morning
comes home
on my father's clothes in the afternoon.

I can't tell my friends where he is working.
'The knackery. Rough as guts,' they say.
Getting out of his clothes, he gives us a hand
with the night milking, leaving
the smell of dead animals trapped in the car.

Summer nights, I ride an orange racer down
to the river, dark waters illuminating
my voice, my father's words
*you've just got to push and shove.*
The churches and milk bar closed down
what we say about each other lives on.

# What the night gives

The white netting on the apple trees
hangs like jellyfish in the night.

Darkness abides yet kikuyu shines
with a struggling jasmine yet to climb.

The netting sways and drifts like a blousy
comment that enters a dinner table space.

The outer reaches of the night, it seems
have been captured between paling fences.

A dog squats. A bat whooshes
from the neighbour's cherry tree.

Juices splattered across our pavers
trace the carnage of their feasting.

Each night they circle, like choppers,
emissaries that live on darkness,

their hunger becomes a fever raiding
the quiet of trampolines, views

from kitchen windows. The netting shivers,
a possum scurries along the fence line.

Stars threaten to fall.

# Across the universe

On the day John Lennon was shot I lay on the warm boards of a country bridge looking between the planks to the river below. The river was more of a creek and the waters were barely flowing. I could see rocks and pebbles below the surface, some reeds near the bank. The planks of the bridge smelled of old wood and some were caked in dust. My sister was lying on the bridge as well, peering down the cracks, filling in time. It was summer and we had more weeks of school to encounter. She asked me why somebody would want to shoot John Lennon. I didn't know and it made me think of the songs on his recent album Double Fantasy, which I had been listening to in the dairy some mornings after milking. It was a much slower album than I wanted it to be. The local radio station hammered Just Like Starting Over while I squee-jeed the cow shit across the yard and into the drain hole. I often wondered if John Lennon could imagine this was happening. He was somebody I had grown up with, taken for granted, like a cousin I once fought with. The creek was barely moving. My sister and I lay on the bridge looking between the cracks to the waters below. There wasn't much traffic on the back road. The tanker had already collected the day's milk. We had the bridge to ourselves. Central Park was in another universe.

# Inner beat

I remember
toe-tapping in a country hall to McKinnon's Orchestra.
A farmer transformed by *Brylcreem* to sing
*Why don't you love me like you used to do?*
Farmers and their wives skipping into a waltz
swapping partners to *The Pride of Erin.*
Laughter, cheap perfume, texture of a bra strap
through a nylon dress. Men watching from the doors,
children watching from hard plastic seats. Flushed face
of a farmer stumbling through a Kitchen Tea speech.
The surge for Johnny Chester and Hotspur.

It was the voice as much as the rhythms of Elvis
that had me staring at the ceiling in a Western District bedroom.
His plaintive, big occasion finales helped me to see
beyond the barbed wire. There was something to trust
like a child who makes comments beyond their years,
a type of wisdom our paddocks received
each night I rode after the cows
belting out *Kentucky Rain* on a motorbike.

I remember
the need to throw a full can of beer at a lead singer,
pace around a bedroom with the stereo blasting before going out
raising a fist to the stadium screens, guitar onslaught of The Saints,
the need to wipe it all out, flailing arms, banshee hair,
Nick Cave taking himself seriously.


After dinner, I chase the focus
a guitar can give. Steve Earle's voice is within me.
The snarl, songs of immigrants, roads

I lose myself to—scrubbing the breadboard,
washing plates, looking for a clean bench.
Something takes shape between the sink and the stereo
some other way of being occupied, lifted.
I look out to fruit trees, roof tiles and poplars.
All my cds have been lived in.

# Ecklin

There are no mansions in Ecklin
no gravel driveways leading to lawn and gentry.
There is Plozza's Road, Lilley's Lane,
hardiplank houses with rotary dairies,
grain silos glinting between stands of bush
clusters of Friesians feeding from hay racks.
There are no hills in Ecklin
just a footy ground with one wing sloping
toward the shadow of a cypress plantation.
A corrugated iron changing room
a history of astute rovers,
a club that folded like a map that wouldn't fold
its creases becoming roads
for school-leavers to flatten it toward the city.
There are no car parks in Ecklin
just people cutting back blackberry amongst the ferns,
afternoons I spent patching potholes on back roads.
There are no mansions in Ecklin.

# Hurtle

Intimidating flatness, mocking blue skies, orange gravel.
I'm sitting on 115 clutching the steering wheel.

A Harry Dean Stanton landscape of wandering, regret,
returning. Travelling brings us together, keeps us apart.

What type of man have I become?
I'm living on a frayed edge of where I belong.

Straight line of a panicked emu
sprinting to join its mate on the other side.

Where red sand gives way to white gravel
I slow down, work through the silences.

My wife asleep, daughters plugged into games.
Just the pummel of tyres, unmistakable argument of horizon.

The kind of driving that cleans me out,
throws me back into the seat, scanning for trouble.

I ride out the kilometres easing into dips,
humming over grids, past branches dumped

around red gums, folds in the sandy river beds.
Looking at the scrub, I wait for ideas to materialize.

165kms to the next McDonalds. Every thought has its space.
Cirrus clouds tearing, our conversations let go.

Land doing the talking, red sandy road unfolding.
I'm driving into country I've never been through before.

# Camellias

I take a straw broom to the damp leaves on the side path.
The concrete pavers are stained and dirty as they have been
for much of the year. Stooping allows me to see
clover around the Mondo Grass—those collars of green
I planted amongst crushed river pebbles by the back fence.
'What was I thinking' is a question often floating in the garden.
I sweep leaves as I go, remembering how long it has been
since I was this low to the ground,
how long it has been through winter
since I have smelt the damp earth,
noticed the buttercups, fallen twigs,
English Ivy slipping between fence palings.
I drag the green bin along the pavers, its wheels
clattering and scraping against the concrete edges.
Squatting to weed, I think of the meal and wine
shared for a friend's 60th, the way he spoke
of making art for the community,
of friends present or absent.
He spoke also of making time to like yourself—
difficult in an over-achieving world.
My back aches each time I lurch for a new weed.
Relieved when they are pulled out easily,
I decide to mow, then collect fallen pink camellias
from the tree by the front door.
They are soaked, turning brown, the edges
mildewed as an apple core.
I place them in a circle around the front garden bed
that is a mix of salvias, Lamb's Ears, Grevilleas
and a sprightly Manchurian Pear in the centre.
The contrast works and I realize it is one of the few
creative acts I have achieved this week—
placing fallen petals around the edge of a garden bed.

Johnny Cash was arrested for stealing flowers.
The Stones sang of the Dead. Perhaps
I will come to notice the camellias in the coming week,
feel the kick as from a recently finished poem—
something layered in doubt but flickering with surprise,
the way one snake story sheds its skin for another.
I pull the cord on the mower.
The neighbours drive past, waving.

# At fifty

I have the freedom to be anxious
about my age, now that I am familiar
with the idea of mortality approaching
like a grassfire. Arthritis, reading glasses,
hanging out with the grey-haireds at the MSO.
Even though, I, like you, can imagine
I am 25—I could do this, could do that—
I don't. I am still an old punk,
an Indian freak, a farmer's son
besieged by superannuation, mortgages, infrastructure—
All the dead nouns lining up to be counted.
Perhaps I have grown up, have my house
in order, have finally succumbed to character:
contradictory, nostalgic, doubtful. My half-baked
ideas sewn, stripped and shaped by family.
What I imagine at fifty ends up as memory.
The past can be cruel as a scalpel to our bodies
yet the constant looking back deepens the present,
the way the bottomless waters of The Big Hole
were always something to kick against.
I'm often distracted, otherplace, need to be guided
into the right paddock, the right cattle track. I'm alive
to possibilities that may not be responsibilities,
the way a conversation on the couch ricochets
through subsequent days or the tone of my daughters' eyes—
a sustained richness I'll take to what the future might bring:
that cloudshadow stretching over a harvested paddock,
this inherited urgency to begin.

# She talks of a future

*For Lucinda*

I catch her in front of mirrors
regarding the idea of herself.
Her posture improving as an act
to keep her hair straight.
She refuses fruit, raids the pantry,
is the last one for breakfast.
She reads while descending the stairs
nimbly stepping over what she didn't put away
from the day before.
She talks of a future, of what she would like to be.
I have fears of boys harming her
girls pummelling this bubble of self
the look she has carefully arranged,
the way she places her chair before the table.
Some days I cannot protect her.

Those early days after school
when she arranged her dolls on the bedroom floor—
the different voices, her female selves,
lined up, grouped, reordered.
This image of herself, of girls, of school battlegrounds.

She opens up in the pool treading water.
Questions float between us—childbirth, marriage,
how she will do things differently.
I want her to swim laps to build self-confidence.
She strolls to the change room
sleek as a bullet, loosed and aimed for the future.

# Cows in India

The first time I saw cows in India
I wanted to round them up.

Yard them, milk them, close the gate
on a paddock, watch them nod along a cattle track.

Instead, they wandered down alleys
up steps, along ghats, singular as saddhus.

They ate what was given—scraps, leftovers,
plastic, cardboard, even slurping their tongues

into huge woks of curries as they shambled
onward, forever onwards. Although,

I have seen a Brahman meditate in the middle
of cyclists, rickshaws, buses and beggars. Unlike

Holstein Friesians, the Indian cow is neither jumpy
or ear-tagged. They possess a quiet that is mundane

as flicking a fly with an ear. I've seen them dead
at roundabouts, have had to back away

from the trembling eye of a water buffalo.
I travelled to India, not looking for answers

just fences, gates, that farm
the cows in India lacked.

Locals even painted their horns blue,
hung flowers round their necks.

The first time I saw cows in India
I wanted to round them up.

# The politics that will drive my own ageing

My father was a Bill Peach man.
After two hours in the dairy, sitting down
to *This Day Tonight* added calm
to the scraping of kitchen chairs, kids
snapping at each other, a dog catching a fly.
Peter Couchman filing his reports in a khaki shirt
got under the skin of Vietnam.
'This is true,' my father muttered
as baby powder floated and steam bloomed
from the bathroom next door.

Fraser instead of Gough
economics over the environment,
my father still likes to provoke with a moral view.
He reads more newspapers than I can in a week,
gathers evidence to stump me with a statistic.
He avoids talkback, has replaced Couchman
with Andrew Bolt. 'He tells the truth,' my mother says.
I bite my tongue, listen and sigh
for the politics that will drive my own ageing.

Up for a hip replacement, my father
has an appointment for his pacemaker.
Full of bluster, 'these doctors are mad.' He makes
it to the back stairs, stands to shoulder
a weight he will not let me see.
I mow the lawn, together, we cut back
some potato creeper, a job
I'm excited by he's planned for days.
I've become the son in his fifties
weaving like a farmer through the lounge room
shonky hips, a niggling knee,
an inherited figure on cholesterol.

He talks of the years left in this house,
keeps a baseball bat beneath his side of the bed,
sits in the front garden hoping to catch
a familiar face walking by.

In her 80s, my mother walks two kilometres
home from the Red Cross Op shop
through the streets she grew up in.
Each Monday, she works the register,
hangs clothes, chats to the women
of her generation returning to independence—
fifty years since her first job before marriage.
'No trouble these days' for my mother
to walk past the bluestone church
her funeral will be said in.
No trouble these days to make a cup of tea
put her feet up, read the sports pages. These days
her generation is falling down in kitchens,
having cataracts removed, in need of respite, lifts to cards.

We sit in our lounge chairs reading with the TV.
My father talks of the big turnout at Mass,
families he tracks on his rounds for St Vinnies
lining up for Sunday night Bingo.
A vicious circle. 'Those Labor shits.'
He rails against the ABC and I wonder
if it is a casualty of ageing—
waiting for someone to argue with.
My mother says she is sick of listening.
He grins at every argument I throw at him.

# THE LOWLANDS OF MOYNE

# She was a Mugavin

She was a Mugavin before she was an O'Keefe.
They owned that farm on the Three Chain Road.
Her father was a great man, like salt and pepper,
he was in everything. When he died, the son
took over, married that Gleeson girl.
What was her name?

How long have the McInernies been milking
at Boggy Creek? Well, she was a Murphy
before she married into the family. Her mother
was an O'Riordan, good people, her father was cranky,
drank the farm away. She gave him her name
and never looked back, reared nine kids
kept her health, sang up the front at Mass.
Like her mother she was known
by two initials on their cheque book.

There was a woman who kept her name
once she was married. She'd insert
her maiden name between brackets
like a correction to what had happened
after her father had given her away.
Once taken, it's hard to go back on a name
like the woman who was a Croft before
she was a Delaney before she became an O'Connor—
each name another point of departure.

# A father's silences

1

'Were you with a girl at the footy?'
My father asks while weighing down on a milker.
His large, freckled hand like a stone on the claw
of the machines draining a back quarter
of an old Jersey reluctant to give.
I lean against a post darkened and polished
by our shoulders. 'No, I was just going
for a walk.' He looks at me, adds, 'I saw you
behind the trees.' My mouth begins to dry
and my heart picks up its beat. 'No, I was
just going for a walk,' I repeat. He shakes
his head, turns back to the cow's flank.
I escape into the holding yard
round up a flighty heifer for the bail.
When our eyes meet
I'm the first to look away.

2

One afternoon he drove me to Terang
to catch the Melbourne train. Early
and waiting, I was struggling to find
things to say. I looked to the red
brick station, the car park, the dashboard,
the radio controls, the heater, the automatic
gear shift lever, found myself muttering
about weather while my father looked ahead
and sighed. A familiar, rising dread was catching
in my breath. 'I've got to go,' I blurted.
There was five minutes to spare.
My father, looking away, said, 'no, stay.'
We faltered with our talk until a whistle
could be heard. I watched him drive away,
slow as any country father who has dutifully
waited for the train, waited for words
to come between silences,
silences I am learning to cultivate
driving my daughters around with their friends
accepting my role, keeping quiet
to avoid eye rolls, cutting looks.
Listening to their pauses and laughter
I think of my father—his silences
were paddocks that hadn't been ploughed before
paddocks it's taken me years to relax in
paddocks I've kept returning to again and again.

# The lowlands of Moyne

Mud darkening the stories
what's passed down

utterances, quips
a way of looking at fences

the dark stretches
a scattering of bricks where a dairy was.

Farmhouses facing narrow back roads
wrecks of Commodores dumped in cape weed

beside rusted sheds. Heavy country you could
fatten a bullock with. A mother into farm politics

and the boot-deep mud around her dairy.

There were three brothers who drank day and night
until they killed themselves.

A mother who burned her house down
before leaving her husband.

A house with a green roof
fifteen kids came out of.

Children walking barefoot through John's Bush
stealing fruit from Faulkner's fence
after getting the cuts in a one-teacher school.

Stories the paddocks give up
like bits of pipe, old whiskey bottles.

Stories that go right back there
to a baby being brought home in a fruit box

a boy cutting thistles for one and six,
a girl walking away from the smell of onions

to a rail canteen at Spencer Street.

Once a week a draught horse pulls a car by rope
through water-logged paddocks.

A family of thirteen
cramped and grinning before Mass

slide around behind the horse
hauling them out of their rain-soaked bog.

In the days before electricity
my father said it was like skiing in mud.

# The violin player

1

She relaxes into the rhythms of her bow, tapping her toes
to Uncle Bill swapping between accordion and
mouth organ; a Killarney reel in a damp country kitchen

she will hum on a bus to the dances
glancing at paddocks, stone crosses of the cemetery
a laughter-charged crowd bound for Saturday night at the Temperance Hall.

She knits her way through baby jumpers
casting on, knit and purl, casting off while a sister
takes the lead with the talk, the cooking.

The smell of the onion harvest on her brother's hands
she absorbs along with his talk of pruning roses,
of looking for an empty honey jar to take

to the Swinton's sale. She has learnt to listen

## 2

sitting in the back seat of a gold Holden Kingswood
in the Younger's department store car park.
Thick-rimmed glasses, silver necklace, pearl earrings

she smiles at the stories my mother gives her—
Uncle Dick in the city, the term I have just finished
the leather seats, her old person smells, gaps

in the talk my mother looks at me to fill.
The hours she wades through, unaccompanied
until her brother and sister return

with brown shopping bags, loaded and particular
while she turns to afternoon sun warming
her passenger window, the local fear of doctors

has rendered her sightless

### 3

sitting by the window of a front room. She listens
to cousin-talk of marriages, clearing sales,
the 1946 floods when she saw the river rise

above sheds, leaving piles of snakes writhing in its wake.
She will never marry or endure a long-term relationship.
Consigned to her favourite stool

memorizing her way to the bedroom, bathroom
how winter sun strikes round a country room,
the authority of her sister, the cunning of her small-time

farmer brother, who would never make a will for fear
of dying. A sister who could once swing a bow, smiling.
Each time I trudged through the car park to the Kingswood

I carried questions about darkness I would never ask her.

# Farmer's wife

Cracks in the clay, locusts flittering over bleached stalks
a woman steals a look from a farmhouse kitchen window.

She married into the district, thin as a whisper
a woman who was summoned to the front rows at Mass.

Wind ripples through washing, paddocks of rye grass sway.
She gave up teaching to smile through luncheons, gatherings.

She made the small talk that fertilized a district.
This year's heifers flicking their tails from the shade of a sugar gum.

Like a rumour she slipped round her kitchen
school forms for children, his phone calls after tea.

Hoof prints shadowing a cattle trough
the farmer who couldn't stop clearing his throat.

A hard doer, priests warmed to him talking a district,
a footy club, the cranky bugger who got things done.

Cypress tree shadows, muddy corner cut by the tanker
he bought up land, kept his neighbours at a distance.

Nerves in her family, shadows beneath her eyes.
He warned her to behave, lay off the grog

she laughed him off. Sheets of corrugated iron
curling from a pigsty. The woman who never touched the CWA

the woman who dressed for his municipal heights,
who drank to his occasions, who stood on the edge

of his name in the paper. They found her in the shower.
The parting statement of a farmer's wife echoing round a district.

# Everything becomes metaphor

*i.m John McKay*

Looking down from the kitchen
into the valley's grainy darkness
I think of my neighbour who won't return
from hospital to imprint his side of the bed again.

A scattering of streetlights gives space
to his absence. Tiled roofs, poplars & magnolias
emerge to confirm the view. I live by what I see.
I remember my neighbour in his Akubra

clambering along with his dog
giving me a startled wave, mouthing a wha?
as I curved past those days I failed to appreciate.
Trowelling beneath pebbles for kikuyu runners

I see what's beneath the urgency of the weekend—
damp clay clinging to the roots of weeds.
The boundaries of the backyard are
what I hunger for, where everything

becomes metaphor, enlivened and random
as hummingbirds drooping from blue Echiums.
Late evening light softens the corrugated zinc garden bed.
Only in memory does the voice of my neighbour begin to glow.

# Hinterlands

What do we feel when a parent is struggling
for breath, for traction on a footpath?
The pull of getting back to them

to change a dressing, clip their toenails.
The care that's unspoken oscillates
through the day—appointments, blister packs,

nagging thoughts. Past arguments settle
into their own terrain.
Things you no longer talk about

the way your parents could never lie,
now you are dropping by, calling over.
The parents who don't want any fuss

keep chocolates two years past their due date
and talk of funerals the way you talk of *Netflix*.
What you will do to keep them alive

in the now, amongst the talk, the paperclips,
unopened mail we never get to put away.
Words we've been meaning to share

but can't think of, like walking into a room
and second-guessing why you came there.
What we see when we read each other's glances

what we feel when we hold paddocks
leveling to the horizon, spaces
razored by memory—

the way grief sentences a man to repeat
the days of his mother's passing.
The talk that circles a death,

when each day becomes an event
to find change for the car park,
days thrown together like serviceable clothes.

I keep returning to gravel roads
somebody else is taking
past shadows from cypress trees

that pull dry cows the length of a paddock
to give birth in, muddy, protected spaces
no Display Home could conjure or promise.

Still, I gain shelter with late night calls
listening to recounts of their days
my voice rising above the remotes and shopping bags

recalling the names that will have them talking
dwelling in the stories that somehow become us,
the waking questions we want someone to reply to.

# The things they carry

*The things they carried were largely determined by necessity.*
—Tim O'Brien

The sound of the streets is the growl of purpose
the six am momentum of fathers and sons
running errands down the alleys and footpaths of a city.

A whine that spirals to a high-pitched roar.
Waves of scooters flowing like oil around taxis,
through roundabouts. Nobody has time for burnouts.

The things a scooter carries—families, teenagers texting,
sacks of grain, a wardrobe, two goats in a basket, a small cow,
whatever's necessary

in a country with a history of invasions
there is no road rage, just polite chaos at roundabouts.
I carry my ignorance, my Australian assumptions

where fall-out from the American War lingers
with genetic disorders, a man with deformed limbs
drags himself across a busy road. Fathers

who fought with the Viet Cong pass their stories
on to sons who lead tours to jungle temples
while veterans wake up screaming at dawn

drink rice wine, beat their wives
until their granddaughters break the circle
talking of abortions, suicides, inherited violence.

The elderly who survive sell lottery tickets from a gutter
while the faces of those who disappeared
we pay our admission price to,

like the massacre at Ben Tre that has become
a place off a back road nobody talks about
except those who are willed to keep returning

with loud opinions and a shoulder bag
weighted by memories of the jungle.
Each morning a rooster crows. A radio station

broadcasts by loud speaker to the streets
what the government is doing. Who is listening?
Like heavy surf, traffic pulsates

outside my hotel window. I look down
to women sorting through hessian sacks
at a rubbish-sorting depot. Other women

fold their histories into rice paper rolls,
sit at markets with a meat cleaver and a tray of raw chicken.
 Meanwhile, men sit on low plastic stools

or laze in hammocks, scrolling.
The things a driver carries smoking on a river barge
steering a path between water lilies,

between the intimacy a woman creates washing
her hair in a Mekong tributary
and the histories a country asks its people to bear.

The things a tourist carries—
a baby's face squashed against her mother's chest.
The father driving without a helmet

their four-year-old son holding on.
His eyes stray to mine as the lights change
I step out before the motorbikes.

# Men I have worked with

The timber worker who looked me in the eye
and said he wanted to understand his mother.

The father who wore white overalls and a hairnet
operating the cheese guillotine for forty years.

The quietly spoken manager who took a long lunch,
called me into the office and sacked me.

The man who ordered a pie, a sav in batter
and beat me in table-tennis each lunch time.

The man who talked with a rollie in his mouth.
The man who talked to himself while picking lemons.

The saw sharpener who gave every tool a place
and tried to give me words of advice.

The man who slept in his bath
when he couldn't find his bed.

The man I caught having a bong behind a stack of flitches.
The man with the DTs running off-cuts through a circular saw.

The short man with the large voice
who allowed me a coffee cup after three month's probation.

The man who argued with his father, the owner
of the business, then walked away, shaking his head each day.

The man who introduced me at after work drinks
to a man who was the bloke to see if you wanted someone killed.

The man who paid for my long lunches
but couldn't always pay wages.

The man who sacked me after a morning's work
because I wanted to stack sports equipment my way.

The man who watered down clear spirits behind the bar
to conceal the bottles of vodka and gin he was giving to friends.

The barman who gave me dirty looks when I caught him
kissing women in the alleyway behind the Bar.

The man who smoked and swore through an interview.
The principal who stepped aside from my interview to take a call.

The man I returned to three times to ask for my old job back
and who still didn't give it to me.

The man who wears shorts in winter, rocks
on the balls of his feet, stands with his legs apart.

The men who sit at a staff table with other men
waiting for someone to begin talking about sport.

The man I learnt to build barbed wire fences with
and the man who has taught me to take them down.

## Ampilatwatja

I drive a red sand highway into blue sky
through the scrub of Utopia
where stark white gums shiver and glow.
I never know what the road will offer.
I misjudge potholes, pass shredded tyres
termite mounds darkening like gravestones,
the torched shell of a car.
Here the language is Alawarrye
I wait in the quiet after muttered comments
trying to comprehend the raucous laughter,
the downward gaze that won't admit me.
My questions are cursory, glancing
as ash being scraped from a roo tail.
I spend my days watching
locals sitting on cars, chatting.
I make up answers to my questions
walking past car wrecks in back yards
reminding me of farmers' sons
who parked each successive crashed car
in a house paddock, storing them for spare parts.
I read of walking this country
that sings between red dust roads,
of explorers, missionaries and songlines.
I see teenage girls barefoot pushing prams
a donkey pulling at weeds.
At the bush tucker workshop
older women sit around nonchalantly
drawing plants with acrylic texta.
The ease of their lines, how they recline
smile, mutter, sigh. It could be a CWA gathering.
I walk the gravel streets trailed by dogs
and the judgements I didn't expect to begin.

Here, where a low sun sets fire in smoky light
I sit on a concrete porch waiting
for the questions to kick in.

# Driving with the West MacDonnells

Flecks of bloodwood and mulga scattered over red sand
I long for your sharp retorts, their familiar force.

I'm driving at 130ks with a mountain range
curling like a breaking wave, its oxide-stained

rocks bearing the blood that light gives.
The bitumen is straight and unrelenting.

The range on my left keeps pace, a story
of red shale packed tight as bricks.

Even though we are two states apart
your morning voice is in my head,

resident, as the high-pitched squeal you give
to dog videos. I'm paying attention to what's due

thinking of you running from clients to supermarkets,
to music lessons, the K-Mart drop-off.

I drive to be alone with you
while four teenage students shout

along to Selena Gomez's *Me and My Girls*.
Here landforms are tectonic, momentous

I'm quietened by the ranges' telling presence
the lemony light of spinifex and ghost gum.

I'm learning to trust the thoughts this road shifts
how absence brings the idea of you closer

knowing what it feels like to stand beside you
in a crowded room, I'm never lost

but now, weathered by distance from your voice
I look to the mountain, this flatness announcing itself.

# Driving to debating

Lights over the rail yards are sparklers
that never die down. *Every day
is a drug test day.* All that's left at Ford
is the security lights, shadows on the pedestrian overpass.
George Pell is refusing to leave Roma
where girls were once named after their fathers
who could, if so desired, sell them at fourteen
into slavery. George is obstinate
as the music I listen to is old, out of date,
timeless. George is of a time that haunts
like a rash, of looking the other way,
of a justice that dare not be spoken of.
        The brake lights of cars have become
pulses within my thoughts. Tim Buckley
launches into *Sweet Surrender*—the epic
confession to bruised love I never tire of.
The shuttered weatherboards of Norlane
give way to the spindly trees of Corio
as empathy hardens like a row of bollards.
George pauses to compose before a camera,
to restate his innocence while families in Ballarat
attend funerals, not Mass. Flash of the golden arches,
lurid glare of a Caltex, George is immovable as The Sphinx
on Thompson Road, unforgiving as a red arrow.
I turn right into the darkness of School Road.

# Forgiven

I have never experienced such devotion.

Within two metres of me, she lays in the sun
her midnight coat, glossy and warm. A low pant
emanates. She raises an eyebrow when I call her,

clambers to her feet, sidles against the cool
of a retaining wall, scratches her back against
low shrubs before slumping to her haunches

watching me oil the faded woodgrain of a garden chair,
a job I've been stretching out over summer days—
rubbing back worn edges, sandpaper tearing at the creases.

She is a thief who steals for love.

Yesterday while I was out, she stood up to prise
the paint brush and rag from the laundry bench.
This morning I discovered them heaped on the deck

just like the glossy travel guides she dragged through a dog-flap
and onto an outdoor table. She rests her jaw on whatever I touch
brushes her wet nose against my leg after work,

dances, circles, runs into garden statues the moment
a dogstick appears. Muscles tensed, jaw dripping
we make eye contact, all is forgiven.

# Heifer wearing a fence post

When she lowers her muzzle to the clover
the post chafes her neck, swings against her shoulder.
No more than a wooden spacer tied to a loop
of cyclone wire strung round her neck.
She wears her post like a cross, bears its weight
its annoying shape for the days needed
to corral a flighty heifer.
Aversion therapy, designed to stop her twisting
through fences, the lone heifer who discards
the herd to freely wander. The same process
we use to justify drowning kittens in a hessian bag,
whacking crippled calves on the head with an axe
watching the cattle buyer jab an electric prodder
into cows reluctant to climb into the darkness
of a cattle truck. In moments such as these
we separate ourselves from the animals,
realise who we are by detaching
from the fear of the cow we are selling.
Like chaining a dog or dehorning a bull
our aim is to contain something wild,
rebellious, a heifer who will twist her neck
to pull at rye grass on the neighbour's boundary,
her fence post bowing the barbed wire
before she pulls back, snickets of orange fur snagging.
She learns to wear her post
as a sailor wears an albatross. Other heifers
keep their distance, shun her affliction.
Each time she shakes her head at flies
the post knocks against her side like a voice
reminding her to pause before fences.

# Dehorning

Twisting the metal nose pincers is a job reserved
for older brothers. Once the pincers are clamped
onto the septum, the cow's head is pulled forward,
twisted to one side, its shoulders heaving against the crush.
The galvanised reo shudders and jars
to each kick, each sudden arse-end shift.
It's simply a matter of clutching the pincers
the way a water skier latches onto a tow rope.
My father slides the blades down
over the curved horn. He leans back, draws
the steel arms together until they kiss.
A severed horn is caught, turfed into a hessian bag.
Soon there will be a pile of blood-smeared horns
some warm, smelling of cow's breath, rank hair.
'Twist the head the other way,' my father shouts.
Blood needles from the stump, arcing
across my father's face, his leather apron.
Crack! Another horn falls into the bag
dogs are sniffing towards. It's a progress
of sorts, protecting the herd from stomach gouges.
My father's mood tightens as the horns pile up.
I look back to marrow pulsing in the skull
the swivelling eye, glare from an animal trapped.
She snorts froth from her muzzle, bellows and groans,
quietens the moment the gate is swung.
There is blood on my shirt, in my hair
in muddy puddles around our rubber boots.
Some cows bolt up the track, others trot
shaking their heads at blood trickling down
into the powdery cattle track dirt.
We squirt some liquid onto the wounds
to staunch the flow, but most cows

escape from the crush bloodied as punch-shocked boxers
their bullying hierarchy zapped; heads lowered
as if they had escaped the smells of war.
Within a day their scarlet stumps will dry.
No longer will they spook when they see the crush
or hop back sniffing dirt beside a stray horn dropped.
The real test of brothers is dehorning a bull—
its horn thick as a fist, close to a ton of beef
squeezed into a cattle race. It takes two
to twist a Hereford's head into position.
The grip on the pincers, locked, here is a beast
that quickens voices, turns each pull of the septum,
into some type of family emergency.
Both horns off, we leap back away from the crush
once the bolt is lifted, not even fences are safe.
My brothers hang on the looks from our father.

# The smell of a paddock

Driving a tractor around a paddock concentrates the mind.
Whether it be pulling a set of discs, smudgers or harrows
large rocks, ditches and skull stumps need to be driven around.
The curves, Buddhist in style, lead you back into the centre
for you are turning a paddock over, twisting in the tractor seat
the way a parent twists to adjust a toddler's seat belt, watching
loose dirt fall away from you until the taste of the paddock
is in your mouth the way dust from a gravel road seeps through
a jammed ute window. A dry, consuming smell mixed
with diesel fumes sweeping back at you.

I follow the line of darkened soil where the harrows have run
watching sparrows flit from a furrow. When there was a head wind
I drove in a compromised position to avoid swallowing dust
except dirty air blocked my nose, closed my eyes. Crosswinds
gave me breathing space yet sometimes the wind just skittered
and swirled around the blue Leyland while the discs clanged behind
like an orchestra tuning up.

In summer, the mix of heat, dust and diesel fumes lulls me
to sleep. I pull up to rest my head on the steering wheel
making sure the tractor is in a gully or down the back paddock,
somewhere out of sight so my father standing at the back door
scanning the horizon for a rising cloud of dust might not be
disappointed. Yet tractor work was a job my father was bound
to praise; days of back-juddering routine to sew turnips and rape,
layers of topsoil billowing towards Heaven, the meditative calm
of steering a Ferguson while chewing over unearthly paddock thoughts.
A harrowed paddock is rich in smells, of wind and loose dirt.
I step down from the tractor and walk across the soft ridges
to simply breathe in the earth. I scuff my boots over a furrow
and like a fantasy, dust pirouettes above me. The smell

of the paddock is the smell of the farm; of teenage isolation,
fence lines that never waver, smells that memory misses,
waves of clay furrows, tilled park land. Layer upon layer of memory
unfolding the turbulence of the ground. Somehow, I've managed
to subdue forty acres, tame its wildness, know its spaces intimately.
I know its corners the way a woman knows her husband's evasions
yet I have lost the paddock I've ploughed and found what it means
to be harrowed driving in second on a half-throttle, dust and diesel
fumes in my face. I cling to where the paddock takes me tracing
a line of darkened soil with the smell of dust following me
like a threat.

# Home

Light suffers to soften; thin ghost gums begin to glow.
I'm sitting on a concrete verandah bedazzled by flies
humming along eyelids, up my nose, in ears, swallowed.
People cruise in dusty Commodores towards the shop at low speed.
Families of women and children scuffing down narrow bitumen streets.
A woman sits in the dust outside her house, a canvas she is working on
spread out before her. A posse of dogs recline in the dirt, wreathing her.
There is washing hanging over fences, the darkness of front doors, engine parts,
kids riding in the back of a ute from the shop.
All morning, council workmen have been tending to the bitumen
their patches higher than the road that trails off into red dust.
Some kids walk home from the shop with super-doopers.
A boy plucks a caterpillar from a host of weeds.
Six pm, bands of light blue and dusty pink above the horizon.
Someone is playing instrumental Country music to the street
a slow, mournful loop that reminds me of Gurrumul,
yet the night unsettles with kids' high-pitched voices, a dog barking,
streetlights sparkling in the dirty light, and further, in the gathering darkness
orange glow of a campfire. The mood after a long talk about Country
the chasm that widens between the South and the North
when a consultant walks into a classroom looking for a pointer.
Six-thirty, security lights of the verandah blink on, notes of a steel guitar
blend with a light breeze that lifts another evening.
I think of Carl Strehlow's final journey along the sandy, silt flats of the Finke
his swollen, Lutheran body shuddering over shale and gibber plains
'the man regarded as a rock, beginning to crumble.' No God could save him.
'Thy will be done,' his son Theo intones walking behind a buggy being hauled
by donkeys towards crimson sand hills in 1920. Meanwhile
a nine-year old boy with dirty, matted hair and a borrowed school shirt
weaves a soccer ball, barefoot, between his opponents' ankles.
He feints, stutters, races over bindis, gravel and weeds of a school pitch
managing the ball with his toe, matted hair flowing, slipping between legs

with the delicacy of something missed, something balanced, something that lingers
like the notes of a Hawaiian country guitar hanging like dust
from the growl of a white Commodore, brake lights flashing
to the howls of dogs, turning in towards home.

# FELDSPAR

# Feldspar

In a dark light, edges of the granite
begin to shine. A breeze is rocking boats
but the blue gums are barely moving.

Through the lounge window, the mountain
looks back at me framed by how I've been
sizing up mountains since I was a child—

of being chased by shadows
inching across paddocks like spilt ink.
The light shifts and the pink hue of feldspar

catches my eye, reminding me
it is not parents who change but the way
we see them age, sometimes uncomfortably.

Sometimes there is only time to think
when my body is in motion, falling into a rhythm
of words, stubbing my toe on tree roots

the swaying farmer's walk. I trudge on behind you
and the lives of people we rarely see
those deaths we learn about on holidays

other camping trips merge with seed pods
on gravelly paths. We step around hollow logs
pull branches away from our eyes

carry the voices of people sometimes reluctantly
like rubbing a wattle leaf between fingers
then dropping it absent-mindedly

words falling and rising with a dirt path
hooked and twisted branches scattered about us.
I follow your breaths around rocks, uphill

to a view where there is no news, no media
and we are not the centre of the world.
The family I have left behind

and what that means here, beyond arrival points.
Feldspar, banksia, swamp melaleuca
drawing me in like breaths to count the day to.

# The parents

Any night finds them earthed
before a stack of Irish CDs resting
near the bottom of the screen.

An eco-system of newspapers, pens,
walking stick, half-opened Quick-Eze
scattered about them. What falls to me

when I look at my father's face—
memory lines scored by skin cancers
his perpetual ageing grin.

He steps bow-legged towards the fridge.
A litre and a half of soda water
blister pack of coloured pills

and he is pushing his chair back
from the table, fox-eyed.
My mother reads local newspapers into the night.

Footy scores ignite her. She takes out
her hearing aid to doze, talk on the phone
'Go on with you, you're a good one to talk.'

My father offers a conspiratorial smile
later, confides, 'she's the best little worker
I've known.'

Subdued muttering from a radio in a bedroom.
Roast chicken, pasta salad, beetroot slices in a bowl.
These images of my parents I carry on repeat.

A lifetime of farming has come down to this—
sitting in an upright chair watching the races
pushing a walker one hundred metres to a milk bar.

All his life my father has stared at boundary fences
now he watches the footpath for a familiar face.
Each day, their victory is to wake, swing out of bed

my parents carry paddocks between their chairs
cow lines trail their glances. They have never flown
overseas or boarded a cruise ship.

Berthed in two lounge chairs, they watch the footy
bouncing off each other like commentators.
They can't believe how lucky they are.

# Sonnets for a mother

### i

She was always staying up late, pottering
around, folding clothes, reading a newspaper
before an open fire. The grandfather clock
swung to a rhythm my mother padded to at night
rising from a chair to put the kettle on.
She always opened up with a cup of tea and biscuits
her hands clasped behind her head
admitting to wisdoms I couldn't prepare for.

Even now with her radio or TV footy shows turned up
I know what it is to sit beside her
listening to the talk that goes on; who's coming down
to visit, who won't be there at Christmas.
All our lives, we've given her so much to stay up late for.
The sound of her voice worth sitting down to.

## ii

She taps hers fingers on the table when she talks
each corrected thought beats like a syllable count.
She pauses, backtracks, draws out her vowels
for emphasis bouncing between forefinger
and thumb—who Auntie Gladys married
the rhythms of her past dancing amongst bread crumbs.

Of suitors, she had a few before getting word to my father
she couldn't meet him on the steps of St Josephs.
Her own father, dead that morning—it wasn't a story,
although once at The Dances she snapped at a question
'no thanks, I'd rather go out with my girlfriends.'
Loyal to St Kilda, she left her job the day she married—
'It was just something you did.' Lost to the back and forth of tennis
our talk fast becoming background music.

### iii

At a young age I learnt that it was better to lie
than to walk down the street imagining I was somebody else.
Once I feigned the flu for a week until you discovered
the bully that kept me sweating beneath the sheets.
I felt like something cornered by a truth I was trying to postpone.
I walked around with my eyes closed so that I might be forgotten.
You listened in between washing and cooking, bearing witness
with a tea towel, dishing up steaks, talking the way families do.

Your voice on the phone brought the paddocks
back home to me. The way you recounted each football match
each brother and sister—checkpoints in a list repetitive as prayer.
One night I listened and cried from a Mildura telephone box.
The next week I drove six hours to watch you folding clothes.
I am who I am, one day I will graduate from you, alone.

# Watching the news

My mother's hands are quivering.
When she speaks, she rubs her thighs, hips
sometimes she forgets, other times she remembers
by dancing her fingers on a table in front of her.
There is a distance between us we bridge
with phone calls. It is like watching the news
imagining I am informed.

Arthritis swells and stiffens my thumbs.
I've lost strength, can't twist some bottles.
Each hand folds in. To stretch
is to push back the webbing, expose
the lines that persist.
My father's hands are calcified, swollen
from years of milking cows or punching wool
from dead sheep. They hang from him like machines
out of use, blotched as old maps. He blows on the corners
when he turns the pages of a newspaper.

Each conversation becomes a portrait of my own ageing.
There is back story to their silences, expected answers
the way my mother stands close to him outside Mass.
They don't want pity, attention or to talk about doctors
but they do.
My father discusses his pacemaker battery with his brother.
It is a bedrock conversation that measures their honesty
by the way they clasp their hands at the table.

Each time I am with them, I become a different person.
I find my way by their politics, side-stepping the bait
I return to shouting with their friends about football,
rain before nosing about my father's rusting tools

his vice, scattered screws. Recently, I souvenired
his Driza-Bone—torn, faded, the coat he wore ploughing,
to get cows and calves in. I look to its smells
of paddocks, tractors, his way of thinking
hanging from a nail in my garage.

My mother's hands rarely form a fist. They are open
to washing dishes, making cups of tea
each simple action becomes a prayerful routine.
What follows after breakfast—light through
kitchen venetians, talkback railing
from a football radio. I watch her lift
glad wrap from a salad, settle for cold meat
from yesterday's leg of ham. This is why
I drive two hours between lockdowns, just to watch her
relaying news of check-ups, who she ran into while shopping
a kitchen table, the only distance between us.

# What I return to and miss

Like random thoughts of the coming week
white cockatoos rise and fall over a paddock of stones.
Out here on the Foxhow Road where the mind is let go
the dip and curve of their scurrying flight
blends with the memories I rely upon for argument.

A single strand electric fence enables Black Polls
to feed beside the road. Next to the cows, a line
of wooden posts recedes into a shallow lake.
This is horizontal country where what I bury
rises to the surface along ribbons of bitumen
with the sun in my eyes.

Crumbling stone wall fences
sacred dwelling sites, stories I haven't heard
isolated roads I drive to be found in.
Townships diminish, dusky salt pans endure
yet like the certainty of a doubt Mt Elephant
manages to hold the paddocks down.

I pull over, take a photo, spear grass whispers in a breeze.
A lone car barrels out of a bend. This is what I know—
this channelled longing, inescapable as a blaze of canola
spreading down to a gunmetal lake.
Yet knowledge is more than absorbing these back roads
or noticing sheep standing on a dam bank's mound.

It's the questions that surface with each escape
from lockdown. The passing view of Mount Myrtoon—
in Djargurd Wurrung country, a low-slung scoria cone
fenced into a paddock, fenced into silences.
I keep looking back to five wind-slanted cypresses

on a distant ridge, the spaces between them confirm
what it is I return to and miss.

# The potato bag needle

Piercing the hessian, pulling the baling twine through
loose cross-stitch, quick tug of the seam
straightening with the knee, another bag
propped in a crooked line by the furrows.

Scooping up potatoes in dark volcanic soil
dirt in my fingernails, dust up my nose.
Stooping and shuffling forward, my future
owned by the stories of picking my father told.

Some pickers could line up 180 bags in a day
I didn't last a week waiting for the semi-trailer
to roll in, eighteen wheels flattening my dreams.
Pick and sew, pick and sew, load up, pick and sew.

I grabbed one end of a bag, a local held
the other. Together we swung each bag
onto the tray, above our heads, then three high.
The driver stabbed at each sack with a polished

metal hook, the same hook he might have used
hay-carting. He shoved them, kneed them, patted
them into in rows before tying the hitch knots
I could never master. Legs jellied, I stumbled around

lifted by the kind of work my father dreams of
propped up in his electric lift chair watching the races
the job ahead of him.
He'll never scoop the black soil of Crossley again.

A rusted curved needle rests on my window sill
copper baling twine threaded, coiled in on itself
like a story we no longer need. To love is to believe
in this bent ornament that once passed through hessian.

# Driving through mallee towns

Straight roads give you time to think
watch wheat fields unroll. Here you know
where the horizon stands: far-off, remembered
the light unrelenting as a migraine coming on.

Behind a row of houses facing main street
is the scrub, Mallee stumps, dry creek bed.
A high school clings to a view of canola crops
the need to escape appears to be generational.

Red brick two-storey hotels closed down
op shops thriving on a street that could be
a stage set. In the hardware store, a line
of rifles, crossbows on shelves, but the threat

is in the flatness you never knew
a mirage distorting the road ahead.
You focus by holding onto the wheel
driven to flee from where thoughts have led

# Bleached paddocks

Driving light of harvested paddocks
light that lifts you, transcends the stubble
dust billowing from headers, a narrow lane
leading to three wheat silos. The skies
are endless or brooding, clouds thickening
from the west. The Hamilton highway bisects
this dreaming of paddocks that stretch
to the white blades of a wind farm,
clusters of round bales sloping about
an empty lake. Summer's heat rises
with the dust and blonde seed heads bursting
along gravel lanes. On windless afternoons
my energies are thwacked, drawn
to the light bleached by childhood walks
to the river, tussocks and rye grass brushing
my shins, thighs, grass dust and seeds
clogging the air. Little did I know that by
emptying the paddocks of hay bales, I would be
returning to the passing light all these years later.
Burnouts etched into narrow back roads, lines
of tyre tread visible on the bitumen.
It's become a thing to decorate round bales
dress them up as Santa for traffic passing the stubble.
Something timeless in these signs, these burnouts
how the paddocks either dry or bake, memories
frizzled by light in late December. Beyond the roadkill
galahs and cockatoos lift and screech, the light
more than nostalgia, shimmers.

# Language of rubs

Uphill, the Friesians are feeding
from trails of silage; bunching up
flicking tails that have been lopped

to a two-foot stem. Music
of their eating, snorting,
sideways grind of a jaw

chewing as they walk
from trail to trail like people
browsing between stalls at a market—

interested, preoccupied, distracted by flies
flicking strands of hay onto their backs
drowsing the itchy spots.

They file off toward a corrugated iron water trough
nodding, rubbing up against a neck
nuzzle of head against head

older cows bullying a heifer back
a language of rubs
I can only guess at.

# Between the pen and the roundabout

Ear-tagged, matted coats drenched by rain
two dead Friesian calves and a near-dead Guernsey
dumped on the roundabout like soldiers left in the mud
in a Netflix documentary.

Three metres from the corpses, two pens of Friesian calves
undercover, hopping in ankle-deep sawdust, ambling up
to suck at my fingers. Each calf is ear-tagged to an A.I bull—
Altamatt, Karma.

Beside the heifers a pen of bull calves
stare into the middle-distance, brooding
as if they know they are about to be turned into steers
by the tightening constriction of a rubber ring.

Between the pen and the roundabout
is a muddy patch of gravel tractors and utes
idle over. A space to watch a cow
returning to the dairy to moan for a lost calf,

a space between the living and the dead
measured by the rise and fall of the near-dead calf's
matted coat, a space where I'm owned by the need to look away.
'It's not often you get three buggers dead in the morning.'

# Between a paddock and a hayshed

The longing begins
      when washing dishes,
places you are called back to
      in the supermarket car park
waiting at a roundabout
      walking out of a fruit grocer
into late afternoon light, places
      that buffet, wash through you
the way a memory scrapes at a residue.

I remember the groan and sway of a trailer
      130 bales stacked and bound.
Rocking to the rhythms of the load
      fumes from the tractor lulling
my brother and I into a stasis—
      ten minutes nodding off to the lean of the axle
floorboards of the trailer
      creaking like old doors opening,
a daydreaming head-lolling space
      the trailer rolling through shallow
grassy drains, hay bales shifting their weight.

From on top, I counted the paddocks on our farm
      ran my eye along the boundary fence,
training myself to read distances—
      those blurred, extended feelings between fence posts.
But mostly, I was clutching at the leaves of passing gum trees
      looking to the treeless hump of a mountain
to see what could become of my brother and I
      sleeping on the job
between a paddock and a hayshed.

# What we did to each other

I used to catch him on my way to the tram stop
sitting out front of his weatherboard in shorts
wheelchair parked on a concrete path.
There were clouds dissolving over the Bay
container ships stationery on the horizon.
He wasn't going far, just across the tram tracks
to drink with locals sitting on stools, smoking
their voices crackling and spitting from throat cancer.
At the time, my job as a sawyer had me on the lookout
for stacks of timber swinging through the air
sometimes at head height. Customer orders
of cut oregon and pine were hoisted by strap
and crane over the bread and butter rows
of eight be twos, eight be threes and ten be twos.
The stamped numbers of 8:25, 8:21 and 5:03
recorded my days as did folded notes
in a manila pay envelope. There was a simple beauty
to stuffing notes into my jean's front pocket
of never being short, unlike the email
on pay week today with its list of numbers
that can't be counted between your fingers.
Each lunch I bought a hamburger and sav in batter
hoping to catch the eye of women in greasy
take-aways skimming eggs from hot fryers
their eyes dulled by steam and scribbled orders.
The timber yard collected itinerants from sawmills
around Jamieson and Yarra Glen.
An old Croatian arrived with a Gladstone bag
sat on wooden benches alone in the staff room
watching me get whipped in table-tennis each lunchtime.
His English was faltering but he had the strength
needed in a tight situation. Each day was a repeat

of tailing out—sliding a cut length of timber
back at the sawyer for it to be cut down again.
One day a length of timber became stuck
in the bandsaw, was let loose at such a speed
the person tailing out was sent flying
back into the wall of the office, a length of timber
impaled in his stomach. After work drinks—
were obligatory as a bedrock of tall stories and unreliable men
who might turn up stoned, hungover or want to fight you.

But not Vinny Meade. He walked back and forward
into his life for eight hours along the sawdust-
sprinkled tracks. I recruited him from the country
hoping he would give into the screech of the bandsaw
sliding eight be threes back at me with a smirk and a ciggie
until it all became a floating dream—sawdust
clouding the air, eyes lifting to a round silver clock.
I learnt how to defeat a man by keeping him on track.
Both of us were like Sisyphus, absorbed by routine
going nowhere and running out of things to say to each other.
He returned to the cows, died too young. I didn't measure up.

Truths and exaggerations were part of the air
I breathed in Port Melbourne. The Painters and Dockers
were always looked after, their orders
rushed through for free.
Most workers were missing forefingers or thumbs.
A rollie helped some people lift something greater than themselves.
One day a saw sharpener was fixing a problem
at the bandsaw. I swung a flitch from a stack
bounced it on a wooden trolley, guided it toward
the bandsaw that buzzed and jiggered
like something uncontained. It was a job
I performed each day, catching a rhythm
with the flitches, balancing thirty feet of Oregon on a trolley
pointing its breadth toward a humming blade.

Something waylaid the sharpener.
I bounced the flitch onto the trolley
but couldn't contain the force of its swing.
The flitch slid to the floor trapping the sharpener's
ankle against the steel trolley rails. His cry of pain
let me know the ankle was smashed. We pulled
the flitch away. He was sixty and never worked again.
I escaped the timber yard with my fingers and the dream
of trying to catch the flitch before it crushed his ankle.
What we did to each other and learnt to look away from
made those days bearable or necessary
as the man in the wheelchair pushing himself
across the tram tracks towards his obligations.

# Taking it slow

      My great-grandfather liked to take things slowly
trailing the cows he bought in Terang back to Warrnambool—
      a distance of 45 kms, all the while walking with his hands
clasped behind his back in the early part of the twentieth century
      a man who fondled potatoes, rosary beads, was noted
in a newspaper obituary.
      My brother and I learned to take it slow walking behind 120 Jerseys
along a back road of ferns and stringybarks, catching their big-boned swaying rhythm
      looking for a dawdling calm, following the leader
into bush country that had mostly been cleared.
      In time, my brother and I came to know the curves and ridges of this road—
when to expect rabbits or an echidna bunched in the gravel.
      We drove the cows 15 ks to Swan's Lane for summer feed, autumn
we walked them back, heavily pregnant, pausing uphill
      from Brucknell Creek where the bitumen rises then drops, our futures
mapped by a herd that was ready to calve.
      Each morning I like to take things slow—
release the pup from her crate, clean her mess
      wipe down the black plastic floor mat.
Each action driven by cause and effect
      following her out the sliding door, across the deck
down the concrete ramp to the back lawn.
      She squats beside an apple tree, a routine that wakes me.
I pour pellets into her silver metal bowl, make coffee
      stroke her back while she sniffs under the chair
I think of my great-grandfather
      walking from Warrnambool to Ararat
to visit his daughter in the *lunatic* asylum. The kind of random thoughts
      I followed sliding blocks of cheese along a conveyor belt—
tracing a pattern with my hands while thinking about something else.
      Twice a year my great-grandfather tramped through bush
skirted the Hopkins, shifted through Hexham, Willaura

   to pay the fees for his *highly strung daughter*
one of many teenagers, housewives, women enduring mania
   of polite disposition, captured in grainy black and whites.
Insignificant, history-less women locked behind peep hole doors
   suddenly visible all these years later through stories I cannot trust.
Where was my great-grandfather taken on those walks to Ararat?
   Losing himself amongst the ferns, the way my brother and I mumbled
to each other, scuffing our rubber boots along gravel and bitumen
   my great-grandfather taking it slow along dirt tracks, his daughter, Minnie,
on laundry or kitchen duty for years, a woman who couldn't look after herself
   dependent on routine to wake her in the scrubbed linoleum wards.
I spoon some peanut butter into a Kong for the pup
   her restless energies, focused, calmed as the morning can ever be.

# Turning my back on Australians overseas

Trafalgar Square, 4am, waiting
for the night bus to Harlesden.
Sober after another night watching punters
drink and shout to the rhythms of thrash metal.
Like any local I step away from a group
of drunk Australians—as soon as I hear
the accent an inner dread begins,
of being reminded what it is I escaped from—
questions, places, assumptions that I will share
the views of backpackers from Kilmore.
Somehow, I avoided cricket, Earls Court
but not the colonial jokes about *Neighbours*.
I left Australia on a one-way ticket
yet the gum trees and paddocks taunt me
as their laughter slips into the chorus from *Flame Trees*
someone's about to chunder. I turn away
as if they were homeless. All I need is historic light
sharpening the walls of monumental buildings
garbos going about their business, the N18 ferrying me
deeper into a one-bedroom flat existence, passengers
dozing off or skinning up, the driver calling out each stop
the Australians' voices in my head, out of whack
with the Danes, Italians and French I wanted to impress.

# Midnight Oil at Mt Duneed

hoodies jeans Oils Ts loud tops piercings swagger
queue to the Merch tent screens goatees grey hair
the banter no aggro just tatts no fuss with the over-fifties
families in puffer jackets camp chairs mothers
with adult sons a scattering of masks men who need to stand
to talk clustering with a three day growth sweeping gaze
chairs rugs crackers kids in Oodies sauntering between
food stalls expectations calamari and chips texting a friend
people converging on the arc of portable toilets downward
glance for a moment the Bunnings world held at bay Goanna
as support slip into the nostalgia of Razor's Edge *Torquay Davey*
a generation reflects The Lady Bay when politics was heartfelt
awakening we stand on sloping ground clutching a can
some of us employed in one or two marriages since lyrics
falling from us like syrup heat of a memory flushing the skin
beneath my eyes realizations catching me like a communion
wafer stuck to the roof of my mouth opening riffs of Solid Rock
has strangers dancing grins of recognition repeat of the chords
all around me men are singing badly throwing arms across broad
shoulders some perfecting the mid-50s sway others remembering
how to shuffle each of us knowing how it is to live within three minutes
of a song where a chorus can hold you as the cans pile up
around my feet we keep our distance in the queue for toilets
burgers or Timboon Ice Cream follow the light of our phones
half-believing hope runs the length of a song corrugated iron tank
crush at the front post-lockdown yelps deep and meaningfuls
with strangers on Shane Warne who remembers the first time
they read Sharon Olds stopped for Fool's Gold insert your own
failing Prime Minister a tall bald-headed man is waving his arms
frantically at the crowd amped acoustic guitars rhythms from
share-house parties what US Forces does to a circle of arm-flailing friends
I'm drinking sly whiskey with tears my body mainlining the kick

and snare outsiders red dirt First Nations we've been riding these
rhythms before simple repeat of da do do do do do do da doo lifts
the crowd each person rises arms outstretched yearning with phones
bodies falling and rising in unison Garret conducting urging the
heaving mass to surge forever upward this unofficial anthem
floating spreading with the misting rain

# NEW POEMS

# Distances

Growing up on a farm
                      I learned to look in distances
squinting at cars barrelling along
                      the Princes Highway
checking two pine trees
                      near the boundary fence
storming down the cattle track
                      away from noise in the kitchen.
My mother's eyes
                      darting between stove, sink and spin dryer
held my look
                      as if what passed between us
was weightless, fluid, a distance
                      she reeled in like dust pirouetting
across a neighbour's paddocks.
                      I also learned to translate
the far-off looks of my father
                      distances that were not vast
but preoccupied with how
                      a cow might sway down a laneway
looks of elsewhere
                      he carried to the dairy, in the car
looks that I too learn
                      to shoulder, lose myself to.

On windless days I listen
                      to the murmur of trucks and milk tankers

sounds that injure and tease
                                  the quiet, rustling grasses.
Magpies and crows circle around me
                                  as if each day is a dance of call and repeat—
the memory of a fox
                        pacing through rye grass to the creek.
There are years that fall away
                              when I look to the darkened swell
of a drain, a stand of ragged pine trees
                              and further north
the mountain I've learnt to dream with
                              not look against.
How rarely, the cars turned off
                              for the gravel towards our farm.
If they did, we either waved or stared at them
                                    the distances between us
becoming the language we speak
                          like the gaps
between what I think and the way
                          bitten-down paddocks sing
like the force contained in where I stand
                              and the sibilant flow
of a distant, weathered highway.

# Roaming

My father steps toward the white Mt Gambier stone bricks
of the Cool Room.

Inside, an 8,000 litre vat costing eighteen thousand
is wedged between plywood walls.

Two milkings and the vat is filled
drained, self-washes before the milk rises and swirls

like memory again. My father clutches his walking stick
defiant against pools of water, tractor ruts around him.

The stick's claw sinks into mud
each of his steps is a type of shuffle

a gamble on the bedrock beneath.
From a distance, I'm expecting him to topple

but I tend to exaggerate. He moves in slow motion
with the grin of the aged

not quite believing what four rough paddocks
could give him. He wouldn't credit it.

He thinks in figures while I collect images—
three thousand for the feed silo, three thousand

for the machinery shed I held my 21$^{st}$ in.
The trusted pine tree from the back paddock

is collapsing, the neighbour's milkers file along
the ridge of the horizon. Neither of us

will pull machines from the cows tonight.
The milkers that have been let out

stand ankle-deep in mud ruminating over a night paddock.
My father, tentative as a statue, looks to the machinery

shed, its cluttered work bench of rusted tools
quad bikes pulled up before a dusty wardrobe

of pipe fittings and a pen of poddy calves
stepping forward to suck fingers

the warmth of their mouths returning years
of static from a mud-splattered cowyard radio

and nights pouring milk warmed with hot water
into a stainless-steel trough.

Their nudging, their hunger, their heads
up against my knees reminding me of my place and theirs.

Each time I look to the silver roof of the Cool Room
some scrap of the past is renewed, then shed.

My father stands with his walking stick rooted in mud.
All he wants is to be allowed a few metres to roam.

# Weather

My parent's bedroom was off-limits.
A room darkened for a child sleeping
in a bassinette beside their bed.

Sometimes I stood in their doorway
weighted by questions. A framed image
of Mary pointing to her Immaculate Heart

musty smells of the dressing table—
face powders, lipsticks, necklaces,
coins and tissues. Dusty surfaces

I was drawn to, if only to understand
my mother, listen to the murmuring
voice of my father.

When a baby woke, my brothers and sisters
raced to smell the baby skin, carry
the baby down to the kitchen for a bottle

of warm powdered milk. Such smells
of intimacy and daily mess held out
against the clatter of rain on our tin roof.

A thrumming so hard we had to raise our voices
or wait for a lull. One night the rain
came in waves, a damp stain

above my parents' bed began to weep.
My father leapt out of bed clad only
in a white singlet and underpants

ran outside to fetch a ladder with
the starless night rushing about him.
Hail stones had piled up between the gables.

Water had banked until its weight
was released through their softened ceiling
cascading onto their bed, yet

their dressing table remained untouched—
a musty record of my mother hovering
before a mirror with a hairbrush.

# The Simpson twin tub

My mother's days were rarely silent.
Her Simpson Twin Tub whirred and rattled
through its cycles, regular and inevitable
as the chugging blare of the dairy engine
our house woke to each and every morning.
The lino underneath the Simpson was split
and exposed patches of damp hardwood floor.
A water-softened stick not only helped her lift
piles of washing into the spin dryer, it was also handy
when somebody needed chasing out the door.

A stainless-steel hand trough with Velvet soap
turning yellow to white in a metal holder was wedged
beside the Twin-Tub. A louvre window coated in dust
was set above the hand trough. My mother could
look out between the gaps of the dirty louvres
to cypress trees bordering the backyard. The spaces
beneath the tree branches allowed her glimpses
of cows filing away from the dairy. It was a reduced view
as if her days were being shuttered between
the opening and closing of the dusty louvres.

In winter, a clothesline was strung up in the laundry
to air clothes that wouldn't dry outside.
The sole toilet for twelve was also in the laundry
behind a stud wall partition. To reach the toilet
sometimes meant ducking into a pair of undies,
a tee shirt or pillow slip on the way through.
There was no door to the toilet, just a floral curtain
hanging down. Sometimes my brothers and sisters
raced each other to the toilet with the loser falling
onto a pile of washing. People did walk in on each other.

I don't know how my mother and sisters coped.
Smells from the toilet wafted into the laundry
fragrances were bandied about but the dank smell
of old sewage pipes remained. Some days
flies hovered and buzzed above the farm machinery
calendar hanging above the cistern. The curtain
was never washed—it was always in use.
I rarely used the Simpson preferring, like others,
to throw dirty clothes onto the pile that spread
across the floor. Some afternoons
my mother had simply had enough.
She closed the laundry door
and walked into the kitchen.

# Fifth avenue

Middle Eastern pop
                    from a hot dog vendor's cart
always holding our daughters' hands
every parent's fear of losing them, the anxiety
you wake to, look out for. Lucky scrapes
in Metro stations—doors beeping, a daughter
hauled inside. Ten minutes of panic inside Notre Dame.
Moods, sensations, I carry with me, keep quiet about.
Sometimes the trigger for memories is the American flag
                    fluttering over a hotel lobby.

Here, the air is blessed with adrenaline.
Office workers tapping on phones, rushing
towards a meeting, a bar, home.
'I don't give a shit.' A man in a blue suit
jaywalks, traffic pauses, honks. A cyclist
darts across.        Swept forward
in a peak hour tidal surge, shopping bags
knocking against our legs, like sharks yellow
cabs cruise the outside lanes. Women in fake
tans caress heels at the lights. The subway
thrums beneath my feet.

Bells of Pedi-cab riders, glimpses
of the Empire State, money being made
as I walk, push, shove. What do we decide
before the flashing silver man? Our daughters
slip into whatever the street promises.
Light smears the Rockefeller Centre, your
inner need to photograph what can't be captured—
a gothic doorway, a rapper swivelling on his head
before you step back to us, flushed by the ordinary.

Night brims with neon
day glow light where all our blemishes
are illuminated beneath news text
streaking across buildings, light
ribboning around corners, dazzle
of Corona, JVL, Coca Cola.
You piggy-back a daughter to save time
to ease the moment
shoulder bag to the left
sweaty palms clasping your neck.
People sit at tables, smoking
non-plussed by the ecstasy of light
shivering around them. Sirens wail
colours ricochet, our daughters' mouths drop
we look up.

# Dreams a daughter lets slip

We live our lives through the dreams of our daughters
some of us fly interstate to watch them perform.
Once they have left, we are the husk of a parent
still trying to get them to stack the dishwasher.
We lend them money for their talk ignites us.

For it's not the driving to dance or soccer
the mother who forgoes the shower
the daughter who stamps her feet pleading release
but the dreams a daughter lets slip—
a bracelet buried amongst beads and pencils in a drawer
a brown hair tie that means so much more.

This morning, I dreamt I was wading through
a field of poppies, you were standing
on a dirty beach, squinting from another age
your dreams arrow-shot, somewhere becoming made.

# Parenting days

Moving our daughters home from their share house
becomes one of those parenting days
of action, to do lists, sweeping dust from under their beds.
A hired van, yellow trolley and the prospect
of shifting their lives west
away from the long walks to the station
away from the IGA and the sense of a city on their doorstep.
This is a day of servo sandwiches and iced
coffee on the run, of bearing the load of a wardrobe
with flashbacks to my own moving days—
it always rained, those radiant promises of a new address.
We grapple with a desk, bow-legged, one step
at a time, resting, then lifting to walk backwards again.
Bulging stripy bags pile up on the weedy lawn
boxes of stuff are stacked on a flannelette-covered
armchair. It's an exhibition of personality
their random desires on show in circles of jewellery
posters, clothes piles and what they haven't managed to throw out.
Leaving a house keeps our talk short—text length
cursory, final as a glance to the Hills Hoist.
Cats in their carriers, a van freighted with what they own
no tail-gating B-Double can upset you—
you are driving your daughters home.

# Rats

I take the dog out, past a glimpse of the neighbour's
widescreen. Rats are scurrying beneath leaves
making a racket zooming along the ridges of a paling fence
fleeing to their underground nest in the vacant block
next door. Terrorists, unseen warriors of the night

climbing up branches to eat the pith of thick-skinned lemons
taunting and mocking us with fruit stripped
and hanging outside our kitchen window.
They leave gnaw-prints in strawberries and tomatoes
lop seedlings, capsicum stems, piss on the lawn.

We avoid poisons, traps or hammers—
instead, we plant herbs, invest in peppermint oil
yet still they nose around the compost
popping up amongst the worms. Each morning
a scarred lemon rests on the lawn
like a grenade someone lobbed.

# Three walks

Two magpies warbling from an electricity pole
wattle birds calling to each other. Flash
of sensor lights, comfort of night light down
a hall, mix of weatherboards, brick veneers—all
renovated and sleeping while I urge my dog to heel.
I scoop up her droppings by car headlights.

It's the hour of partners in tracksuits
terriers, a dachshund, headlights turning
on a street-lit corner, morning light emerging
between the fronds of a Norfolk Pine.
Rhythm of my shoes on a wet footpath
taillights of a car pulling away, all this
before the working day.

The dominion of a streetlight's glow
tradies walking toward a new build in the dark.
Porch lights flecking the ridge of Wandana Heights
dark silhouette of a lemon-scented gum tree
shadows of other dog walkers. The breeze
picking up. The day ahead of me
the sense of never catching up, of just being pulled
uphill by a dog twitching at cars, a distant Retriever.
A man on a chair outside a new brick unit checks his phone
bids me good morning.
A line of heavy cloud behind me
three walks I return to like a mantra.

# Visitors

White cockatoos screeching across rooftops
across the bitumen and kerb of the estate's
empty lots.
A squadron traversing grey light.
A loose diamond unifying the day—
the dream images we long to keep.
They return in waves, circling
our backyard gum tree as if pursued
driven by memory
their Hitchcock energy
wakes me each morning at 6:30.
I drag myself to the sliding door
catch the last of them flapping.
On weekends, a neighbour's gun shot
splits them.

# Joan Eardley

Joan Eardley painted on hardboard facing the sea
a matter of steps from her stone cottage.

A smudgy sun in a leaden sky hanging lost
above snow-filled streets, other times

a swathe of yellow and orange for a stubble-field.
Mood and feel of a scene, scratching and scoring

mixing flower seeds and gravel as medium.
She was moving toward abstraction with

a house paint brush at the end of her hand
her arm arcing and sweeping across the board

catching the energy between paint and thought
the board cut down into a square so that

what she saw, she painted—waves rising and flattening
beneath her, the North Sea churning its grey

stony presence. Storms and light, great blocks
of darkness above and beneath scraps of white.

Sometimes she finished three paintings in a day.
She wore men's clothes, rode a scooter,

spent many nights alone writing letters, grinding pigments
living for an art that might save others.

These days I need something to bang my head against
some boundary, wall or level of self-doubt.

Instead of hardboard, I rewrite A4 Spirax pages
working the gap between first thought and draft.

It is said Eardley anchored her easels to the ground
with stones and pipes. Squally gusts could fling

a canvas one hundred metres.
Paints and palette knife at her feet

she seemed happiest watching the gap
between hardboard and sea. An outsider

who scraped at what the wind allowed
living alone in a stone cottage at Catterline.

She painted until she could not see.
At forty-two, she was dead from breast cancer, 1963

the year I was born, it seems pointless and necessary
to cross out and fling words for Joan Eardley.

# Summer's abandonment

Empty stores in the quiet arcade
white floor tiles stretch the walkways.
Full length windows with *For Lease* signs

the kind of arcade that makes you rush
to the car park, an arcade of hard surfaces
as in any rural town you pass through

yet its ghostly presence lodges in your memory.
Somebody works here, somebody thinks of leaving
the faded shop frontages, dated paving

the Coles superstore that takes up a block.
The anomaly is the Botanic Gardens—tree plaques,
curving lawns, a Monet bridge over a swamp

in a town founded by early settlers, nearby
massacre sites, where the cemetery is sectioned
by religion, vacant blocks extend between houses

and the heat bakes any thoughts of lingering.
You walk around the shallow lake—find yourself
before a map of deep cracks in the grass

a deepening darkness that belongs on a farm
says as much about the town as the gravel car park
where locals hang to eat take-away before ducks.

Out of town, there is stubble, long gravel driveways
a gathering sense of stillness that's not loneliness
country people accepting summer's abandonment.

# The snaking accuracy of cow trails

At 7am I'm listening to crows
reading a low-slung mountain

a line of cypresses climbing its slope.
I'm always returning as if in an endless loop

seeking attachments the Buddhists say I should
release yet my thinking is never still while walking

these paddocks more cleansing than a catholic Mass
even when the tracks are flecked with dry cow shit.

Just as there is a ritual for getting through an electrified
fence, I've snaked under bottom wires to avoid

the shock up the arm, there is a breath I've been
chasing, a way of getting the cuffs of my jeans wet.

Two ducks lift off from the river flats calling to each other
while I'm caught out by the snaking accuracy of cow trails

spreading out like arteries from a concrete trough.
Each winding trail—no more than a foot wide

descends into knee-length rye grass revealing
the path cows might take to the creek, better feed

how they read the paddocks, those flattened patches
where they have lain. I follow such mysteries

drawn by what I might have known of
dock weed and thistles. What's driving me

here is not as explainable, although the evidence
might be in the used-to-be's,

that other layer of thinking beyond feedlot farms
and shouted orders from a car window, stuff

there is no escape from yet here there are dark, cool
spaces beneath cypress plantations, memories surfacing

of cypresses shadowing the old weatherboard.
It's this geography that buries me

as if the paddocks are embedded with cow trails
and that steep grassless hill I drove a tractor and trailer up

loaded with hay bales, front wheels of the tractor
lifting, steering lighter, I gave the tractor some throttle

stood up astride the seat in case I had to jump
a trailer load of hay tipping and rolling away from me.

# Storm cell

Light rain blows over the van.
The pole supporting the bed is creaking.
Wind buffets our talk. Corners
of the canvas are beginning to soak.
Your face lifts at a Labrador walking down the road.
I step out to tighten the guy ropes.
There is a fear in your voice I cannot contain.
I hammer in tent pegs, but the flys are lifting
juddering. Nothing about the van is certain.
Sky and sea are the same metallic colour.
A storm cell of 100 k churning winds
colourfully displayed on our phones
is approaching. Outside, a tent has been
tossed away.

At 4am, rain pummels my face
visibility about a metre.
A wind gust scoops up the awning
is about to hurl it against the van.
Somehow, we manage to hold it down
wind it home with a series of shouts
gaffer tape fixing, rain-coat flapping
harried moments. Weather thickening
around us. Smells of wet canvas
water seeping onto our bed.
Anything fixed groans and sways.
You move to a blanket on the couch
while I lay in bed, hunted and under-prepared.
All along the coast, storms are circling
mould is forming under our bed

# Hard worker

He waits for what you have to say
choosing his moment to slap you

with a put-down, to show you up.
There is a tension between what you might

say and the memory of what he has been.
You have nothing in common but small talk

around BBQs, a returning sense of unease
you can't always avoid. You've moved away

from the jokes he makes about women's tits
the way he looks at you, smiling as if conversation

is another way to set a trap, test you.
The safety of football to talk about

of choosing the right words, as men
often do, skirting along the surface, avoiding

the gaps between what you are thinking
and what you remember—his ability

to snap into a yell, dismiss a woman
because 'she won't shut up.'

He doesn't laugh but grins as you make up questions
waiting for you to run out of things to say.

He's the uncle you inherited, the cousin you tolerate
every comment is a look away from a punch in the face.

# The boys

talk of football, work and piss
taking the jet skis for a run at Lake Hume
the school they went to.
A brother walks in plonks a dozen Coronas down
sits on the deck with the boys beaming from grey cushions
while their wives and daughters plate up.
They take the piss complaining about the sun,
workers who turn up late and expect to be paid.
The wives sidle up after lunch, rest pink nails
on a hairy thigh, a comforting palm on a shoulder.
They agree the Prime Minister's a dead shit
but nobody laughs without sunglasses.
They know how to scoop up a prawn
on their way to the dunny, how to pull a limo
on the drive up to the G.
The empties line up behind a cane chair
their second wives make conversation—
each has a husband's business to compare
a babe to keep jobs, quotes up to date,
their kids overseas school trips.
The boys glance to feeds, scores, bets, hashtags
whatever catches the eye, those nights at Sexyland
Grab a Granny night at the Local, wives rubbing
their lower backs, the boys comfortable
with being affectionate in front of each other.
They caress their wives' knees, thighs,
talk of dumb pricks they have to deal with.
While lip gloss is reapplied, the boys perfect the look
that arises from a session on the deck—grins
to fall back on, thongs to kick off.
Sheepishly, they ask if their Beemers can have a sleepover.

# Archway

Two overgrown cypress trees bending towards each other
a gateway apart, wide enough for a family

to drive a car through into Sinnott's paddocks and further
to a farmhouse. Tyres rolling through strawberry clover

after Mass, every Thursday shopping, kids opening
and closing wire mesh gates. No dirt tracks, just a

worn outline, a palimpsest of a draught horse
pulling milk churns on a cart to a roadside stand.

Sometimes ponies were ridden between the two trees
to school, tied up in the yards behind the big building

now a memory, the school yard reverting to a
space in a paddock surrounded by wavering gum trees.

Whether it was a draught horse or ponies, the archway
was an entrance and an exit, a grand passageway

for two sisters leaving to work on rail station canteens
brothers riding pushbikes four abreast along back lanes

to the Pictures. A family of thirteen finding their way
between kero lanterns and candles, living on rabbits

washing the teats of cranky heifers, pulling wool
from chicken wire fences with 'the War still on.'

Two ageing cypress trees along a fence line
framing a view that pulls me up smart.

What my father remembers I seek to continue
here is the space a Hudson was driven through.

# Fifteen dollars

We arrive at the nursing home while my auntie
is at Mass. After letting staff know, she is wheeled
around to meet us at her table in the dining room.
The tables are beige as is the floor. There are colourful
posters for exercise classes and the kitchen calls itself
a Diner. My auntie is one hundred and doesn't give
anything away. She rarely speaks, preferring to sit
and look ahead. My father tells her the news but
she isn't bothered. She is thinking. She doesn't wear
hearing aids, asks us to repeat what we say.
At one hundred, she isn't easily impressed. Today
she is colour-coordinated—purple nail polish,
purple flannelette shirt, purple cardigan.
She asks after one of my sisters and 'is Mary still driving?'
It doesn't matter. My father is happy to see his sister.
It's been some weeks, including his own hospital admissions.
He's been talking about this visit for days. We sit in the dining room
waiting for his sister to speak. It is a quiet we are duty-bound
to turn up to, sitting at the table either side of her.
Other people start arriving for lunch. Some are wandery
and shuffle back down the corridor before they are brought
back clasping the hand of a support care worker.
Eventually, people make their way to their position at a table.
They sit down, carefully arrange cutlery, unfold their napkin.
One man scratches his chin, deep in thought. A staff member
approaches my auntie with Holy Communion. Instinctively
my father and her bless themselves. A brief prayer
and she accepts the wafer in her arthritic fingers
swallows, washes it down with water from a plastic cup.
She seems relieved, almost at peace before lunch.
A woman is wheeled in on a low bed talking loudly
about her life and the people she doesn't like. She breaks

into The Pub With No Beer, singing verses perfectly in
a broad Aussie accent before she is wheeled out again.
My father rises and my auntie asks if he has any money for her.
He takes out his wallet and I slip out the last notes he has—
fifteen dollars. I help her place the notes in her shirt pocket.
My father says she has a drawer full of notes in her room
from all his other visits. A lasting value for a woman
who squatted on stools to milk cows during the Depression,
who worked on rail canteens and whose fiancé died from cancer
before they could be married, a woman whose fingers have shrunken
and her engagement ring sits in her drawer, a woman we leave
sitting alone at her table, thinking.
She thanks us several times for visiting.

# Circle work

We take our dog to the park by the water.
She sniffs around posts, casuarinas
on the long lead yet looking back
to check in as we are at week's end.

Other dog walkers stride out, ear-budded
their dogs arcing around our slow talk of work,
ageing parents, where our daughters are heading.
We know what each other's about to say so

we circle back to the river darkening
in failing afternoon light. A stretch
of water opening us up to school rowers
bending to the crackle of a loud hailer.

Some harmony to the week you are trying
to measure. A workmate's nights more
telling than productivity data, conversations
you carry for days, turning over.

We lead our dog and are led by what we agree,
decide upon. We pass a homeless person's tent—
work boots outside, plastic bottle strung between
trees. It reminds you of the woman

sleeping rough near your work, the woman
you pass after night shift, her bed in a car park
corner. We carry what we witness, follow a grinning
dog back to the car, back to the week that was.

# Inheritance

Three-month-old calves in the house paddock
watching us hold our arms out, luring them
to step toward the fence line.
Each calf wears an ear tag of the bull they are bred from—
2248 Ponder, 2272 Booyah.
Some rub up against each other's necks
one calf licks another's eye. More calves stand back
shadowed by a cypress plantation, watching, slowly
stepping closer as if they are under a spell.
One sudden move and this cobweb thread of trust
will be broken, the calves will turn, disperse.
My fingers stretch over the fence into childhood
as if I could reel it in, a rope of memories I latch onto
yet feel slipping, dispersing. One dark-coated heifer
raises her head, her pink tongue curls up, around
her nose. She opens her mouth, begins sucking
a gentle squelching like shaking a post in a boggy
paddock. I feel the rim of her teeth, warmth
of her tongue fastening, while two calves step
over to you, sucking your fingers. With an iphone
and a broad urban grin, the two of us taken out
of ourselves, an innocence shared
this fragile connection you have inherited—
a line of calves standing at the fence line.

# There, there

The lanes on the freeway diverge into sweeping bends
red glow of taillights, a wall of warehouses. In the flight
from the city, drivers find their pace, some swap lanes
or slide across three before slinking off to Hoppers. I'm
holding on, my father reclines in his lift chair, breathless,
my life seems to be driven by songs, narratives that sweep
me, whatever the mood. Keeping to the middle lane I begin
to stray, thinking of you on the couch, or washing dishes
texting, something my father never managed. House lights
in a paddock. I remember the country quiet, a mood
I fled to escape from. Ageing seems to be learning to
accept, different thoughts or the undertone of thinking
while staring ahead yet with this thrum of the car engine
I'm reminded of the noise of the TV left on, those jagged
black lines and static that woke me, had to turn off
like the news of a school friend's death undercutting a week.
Headlights loom in the rear vision mirror, speed cameras
I invariably miss, confined as I am to mumbling with the songs
in the middle lane. There's roadwork glow, a service centre
two kms ahead. My father needs his oxygen, accepts each night
flattening into a cloudy darkness. I need music to think
without boundaries, to let go, float off. A crunch of guitar
chords rise. Two lanes glide past the turn off to Lara.
I know what I'm driving into, how to follow white lines
curving down into the valley of Hovell's Creek. My father's
raspy breaths, finding their place the way a song can keep you
on hold.

# Blown showers

A light mist hangs above the paddocks
a familiar greyness through the trees.
Blown showers fleck potholes and gravel
a constant tapping that wavers and builds.

A familiar greyness through the trees
that drives the memory through the mood.
A constant tapping that wavers and builds
daydreams and doubts turned over on a walk

which drives the memory through the mood
and heifers bunched up facing in out of the rain.
Daydreams and doubts turned over on a walk
still the wind groans and scatters bark from the trees.

Heifers bunched up facing in out of the rain
I'm thinking of the rainy paddocks I grew up in
still the wind groans and scatters bark from the trees
only the muted colours produce the lines that give.

I'm thinking of the rainy paddocks I grew up in
dreams of walking the back way before it was gravelled.
Only the muted colours produce the lines that give
all I need is a glimpse of two feet sticking out of a cow.

Dreams of walking the back way before it was gravelled
I drive past muddy gateways, always looking back.
All I need is a glimpse of two feet sticking out of a cow
rain gusting in waves toward a cypress plantation.

Low clouds have smudged an outline of the mountain.
A light mist hangs above the paddocks.
I pull over, turn off the engine and listen
to blown showers flecking potholes and gravel.

# Walking the cattle track

Those low sheltered spaces beneath cypress plantations
where grass doesn't grow and the cattle track
hardens to the consistency of a cricket pitch.
A dry sacramental place where cool air whispers
beneath the outstretched limbs and Friesians sit
chewing, swallowing, eyeing off the day.

Elsewhere, the aftermath of recent storms—
snapped branches hanging from a sugar gum
limbs suspended in forks, saplings
upended and clinging by torn bark.
A pine tree I used to walk towards
has been shredded by north winds.

I walk into the past and write into the present.
The fireballs and scorching winds are a kind
of discordant music to the slow lean of a fence.
Memory is a mash-up of longing, forgetting and
what is always there—rustling in a gum tree plantation
thatched hoofprints of cows drying in mud
the illusion of walking on air.

# Caring pantoum

'If I can get myself up out of the chair I'm doing alright.'
Like a communion wafer I place the tablet on his tongue
he tells me it's like a monkey being fed in a zoo.
Ageing is when you rely on others to move you around.

Like a communion wafer, I place the tablet on his tongue
hook him up to the oxygen, drape a blanket over his legs.
Ageing is when you rely on others to move you around
he calls in the night to wet his throat with soda water.

I hook him up to the oxygen, drape a blanket over his legs
friends call in to share a laugh, he cries when they leave.
He calls in the night to wet his throat with soda water
his feet are swollen and his legs are cold to touch.

Friends call in to share a laugh, he cries when they leave
each day he mutters 'there is somebody worse off than me.'
His feet are swollen and his legs are cold to touch
he begins each day with pickled onions, sliced chicken on toast.

Each day he mutters 'there is somebody worse off than me'
even when he stops the walker to hold on to a handrail.
He begins each day with pickled onions, sliced chicken on toast
extends the lift chair, settles into the races from Mornington.

When he stops the walker to latch onto a handrail
I stand behind ready to catch what this man has meant to me.
Extends the lift chair, settles into the races from Mornington
he talks in short bursts, every word is felt in a breathless urge.

I stand behind ready to catch what this man has meant to me
when I leave, he grips my wrist with two hands, fixes me with a look.
He talks in short bursts, every word is felt in a breathless urge
'once I get myself out of the chair, I'm doing alright.'

# Drover boy

In the dawn light, he starts at the Rosebrook bridge on horseback
collecting cows from house paddocks and stockyards
rounding them up for farmers sleeping off hangovers.
A Jersey here, a Friesian there, twenty-five cows
swaying their hips along the Princes Highway.
There were fewer cars then so he could own this road
by *going up the guts* towards Koroit.
Clatter of hooves on bitumen, one or two dairies firing up.
At fourteen, he knows the back lanes of Moyne, Kirkstall and Crossley
will get him there, and wherever he is going
he will be guided by the names of Lenehan, Farley, Mugavin
names embedded in the paddocks like a muddy track
to the dairy or a neighbour's story that has to be retold to be believed.
Droving teaches him how to read a cow
follow their condition, their walk and how much
he wants his own paddock, his own way of marking the land.
Lenehan, Farley, Mugavin and Gavin—names
he would whisper in between raspy breaths as a much older man
finding his way back through the paddocks
long after the people had gone, but in memory
he could continue. Names he could follow
be delivered to, wherever he was going.

# The roster

Large families in the country were designed to take over the farm
to supply milkers, harvesters, somebody to swallow dust ploughing.
This family of ten fills a roster to care for a father
writing our names on a day in the blue diary
checking a Spirax notebook for weight, diet, extra tablets.
Some of us drive three hours to stay overnight, others swing round
five minutes away or ride a bike through successive roundabouts
to be there with the man who only wanted to have a pitch with others.

A Palliative Care nurse calls by, but he is *perfect*, the day is *beautiful*
he is ready to s*hift Australia*, talk up The Blues, let rip with a political view.
Each day is a routine that keeps us anchored—
he reclines after breakfast, stretches his legs out.
I drape the fluffy grey blanket over him, followed by the Blues rug
loop the oxygen cord over his ears, fix the nozzle to his nose.
It helps to have something to do when your father is dying.

Each of us has our own reasons
sometimes it's a phone call that compels us to catch a train the next day.
Family news is always worst when furthest away.
The roster brings my brothers and sisters closer together
then scatters us with our private thoughts that wake or silence us.
It's what the dying do.

We cluster in hallways, back rooms to debrief, talk in grabs,
our rush to help out driven by the care adrenalin.
A rattle in his breathing has us on high alert.
My father's farming world has shrunk to the rooms of this house.
He talks whispery between breaths.

One morning he swings out of bed buoyant, joking, ready to shuffle to his scales.
He grabs onto a chest of drawers for support.
His weight is up but he can't step down.
I grab a chair, but he drops sideways, slips out of my arms to the polished floorboards.
It is a fall many of us have grappled with in the bedroom
on the sloping concrete path to the front door.
The father we looked up to suddenly down below us.

He never wanted a nursing home, nor to be revived if he was felled by a stroke.
He often told me, matter of fact, he wanted to be let go, if it came to that.
His insights into dying were sometimes frightening.
We paid him back with a last wish, surrounded by family
songs and stories, a decade of the Rosary in between the tears.
Mum held his hand while his breaths gurgled like a tractor climbing uphill
then the exhalations became fewer, as if each breath was being
considered before ebbing from his body. We checked his pulse
arms still warm, the urge to touch, hug him
as he had touched us with his steady look from the lounge chair.
We let him go in his bedroom by a busy road.

# Coolum Beach boardwalk

Along the dark, stained hardwood rails, memorial plaques
have been attached for people who have known
the boardwalk's views of Pandanus trees, surf club, choppy breakers
the family time it had given them.
Anonymous lives memorialised by name, date
sometimes a heartfelt sentence set out on a silver metal plate.
I think of my father, recently departed—
volunteer for St Vinnies, fire brigade, football club, Catholic church
a father who was the fixer of his brothers and sister's lives
who also mended my own. He knew when to give me a job.

Each day his face is in my mind
a presence that comes to life in photos
his sayings that cannot be contained
by a name, date, silver metallic writing.
They live on—jokes, quips to embellish the moments
I have to remind myself, he is not here, but is
like that dark shadow we saw surfacing amongst the waves
wow of its tail thumping the water,
something glimpsed, forever felt, a story
that lingers long after the telling.

# Finding pieces of my father

Bits of rubbish flying off
the back of a trailer going to the Tip.
I'm following the pieces of my father
being blown back towards me.
*Mongrel, freemason.* I'm trying to catch
all the bits of him that I've missed.
Somebody should have tied him down.
Dust and copper strands of baling twine
cardboard flaps, rye grass heads, daisies and jonquils
swelling and spiralling up into a smoke-stained sky.
Whoever is pulling this trailer is hell-bent on Tip Road.
Each time the trailer jolts over a pothole
parts of him are released—his looping, cursive
farmer's notes, U.D.V clippings, it's like
swatting flies, trying to catch what's out of reach
and the way some memory will rise above the thickening dust
doesn't help me understand him, his voice
slipping away like water into a recurring dream.
I'm chasing what's left of him
with the questions I've been meaning to ask
curling like scraps of singed newsprint about me.

# And still the wind moans

We leave head torches on the dresser, part-waxed candles on a bench
go to bed early, storm-threat in our talk, a dark night wavering.
Soon the towering Pittosporum is shaking, high branches rolling
and swaying, scraping the gutter as twigs are hurled skyward.
By two am, the sky is roaming, windows are shuddering, wave
after wave of gusting rain hammering the roof, tin awning.
Rain has become horizontal, slanting through the lemon tree
soaking the deck, pummelling a row of salvias. The noise of the wind
is the roar of a plane overhead, unleashed, it barks and rasps at the house
rushes across the backyard bending a peach tree while a frission shakes
through the Lilly-Pillies.
I stare at the carnival outside, awed and in fear of such force
in my pyjamas. The kettle burbles. Is this the storm my daughters will inherit?
This wind has a voice and it won't relent. Things are being slapped
against the paling fence, the shade sail is being lifted and thwacked
yet the chains hold as if such things are normal.
Daylight reveals our weedy lawn strewn with leaves, branches
a plastic water bottle carton. No tree came crashing through the tiles
no outages, yet I carry the storm images of other homes
looking for damage, the air, electric with possibility, smells of wet earth,
other people's lives upturned and still the wind moans
as if prevented from going elsewhere.

# Barmah

The late light through the trees
glint of a car through scrub on a distant road
timeless quiet of looking beneath leaves to flowing waters
before a screech of cockatoos, semis rattling over the bridge
in Yorta Yorta country of crickets and frogs
their staccato rhythms trilling the chat that never ends.
Tree roots hang from the clay banks festooned with
fallen trunks. Grey branches spear the air. There are signs
that limbs may fall without warning so we take our chances
under a stooping red gum watching the river send out
little whirlpools each time the khaki waters roll into the bend
as if the river was constantly springing back into its flow.
Our job is to comb for twigs and leaves, follow the questions
of gutted fish in the dirt, a nightly ritual to prepare for the fire.
Earlier, a dog reclining in a passing Tinny left us in its wake
showing us how to settle and accept, left-overs
and last night's stars poking holes in the dark.

# Author's Note

The poems from this collection draw from my published poetry books with the exception of two early chapbooks: *Bare Me Days* (1995)—a limited-edition self-published poetry collection with the book bound in paperbark— and *Mungo Poems*, (1997) Soup Productions. The poetry collections that this book draws from are: *Why I am Not a Farmer, A Paddock in His Head, A Tight Circle, Travelling Through the Family, Smalltown Soundtrack, The Lowlands of Moyne* and *Feldspar*. I have also included 30 new poems. It has been a challenge to review each poetry collection and omit poems for this book. Mostly it has been done to avoid repetition of subject matter, to take out what I consider less-realised poems, and poems that, if given the chance to rewrite, I would change and possibly lose in the process. I have often felt that each poem that I have worked on has a life-force or spirit within it. I don't mean this in a mystical way, but more that the poem often asks to be completed within a short time frame and then be reflected upon for a longer period of time. Sometimes, I have been happy with this process, other times I have seen flaws in the work, be it word choice, tone or lack of exploration. Often the poems that I write begin like arguments with myself. Each of my collections has included some less-realised poems, and I believe this is common for many poets. There isn't a secret formula for realising a poem, and I am often surprised by what remains after I have written one. I generally write by discovery, writing about what I don't know, although at times I will think of a title before I have written a particular poem. I rarely revise older poems once published, preferring to see them as examples of what I was thinking or working on at the time.

I have organised the poems in this collection chronologically from publication, ending with the 30 new poems. This may be seen by some as unfashionable or a traditional approach to collating a new and selected poems. However, due to the nature of the creation of my poems—which are often drawn from experience, felt experience, hence the title—patterns should emerge for the reader as they read from the first poems taken from *Why I am Not a Farmer*. I came to writing poems in my early twenties and while I often felt that I was writing in the wilderness, it was only when I began to write about my country upbringings that the resulting poems appeared to take on a life of their own. Although some readers might assume that I had found my subject matter, I remember I was only trying to bring to life aspects of a rural life that I had not read about within Australian poetry. A realistic depiction of dairy farming from a rural perspective is what drove my interest in the early poems. It was the life that I believed many readers didn't know about, and so I have found over the years that many readers, especially country readers, appreciate hearing about it.

Aside from poems about cows, and the often harsh treatment of cows within the dairy industry, as well as the physical effects of farming upon people, other patterns that might emerge for readers include: many personal poems about family (notably my parents); paddocks; masculinity; driving, and a number of portrait poems. That these patterns repeat through the collections shouldn't suggest a limited view of the subject matter, but rather that the ideas and prompts to write often mine territories that seem to me, to some extent, inexhaustible. And yet what begins a poem for me has often been part of a consistent process, one which I assume is common to many poets. I keep several notebooks and a diary from which ideas, images, lines are written in pen. Often the form of a poem will suggest itself to me as a strict form such as a sonnet, a pantoum, or a poem written in couplets or stanzas. The writing of a first draft is often quick, sometimes driven by that image that comes to me in the shower, waiting at the traffic lights, or on a walk with our dog. Sometimes this 'vomit draft' needs to be carefully shaped into a form that suits the poem. I also write and edit by intuition, by what feels right and what looks right the next day and the day after. Sometimes I only realise the form for a poem through successive drafts. This is the part of writing poems—the crafting—that I enjoy but which can still result in a poem that doesn't take off, or a poem that seems to have a life of its own. There is no secret AI formula to writing poems.

In the past, some of my poetry collections have been structured into sections to help break up subject matter, poetic focus or tone for the reader and there have also been sequences that I have written to examine a subject matter more closely. Due to restrictions of space I haven't included any full-length sequences in this book. However, I have included one poem from the sequence 'Towns of the Mt Noorat League' from *Small Town Soundtrack,* and two poems from the sequence 'Songs of the Clay Mound' also from *Small Town Soundtrack*. Similarly, I have included two poems from the sequence 'Driving' from *Travelling Through the Family.* For readers interested in reading the full-length version of these sequences both books may be able to be purchased online, but not through their publisher. Like many poets, other collections that I have written which are out of print are *Why I am Not a Farmer* and *A Tight Circle*. However, *The Lowlands of Moyne* and *Feldspar* may still be purchased from their respective publishers. While one reason for creating a new and selected poems is to bring poems out of print back into a collection, I have found the most rewarding part of the process has been to review the collections, remember what it felt like to write particular poems, recognise patterns that I was not aware of and, in some ways, to understand the types of poems that I have been writing over the years.

Perhaps I have been drawn to writing narrative poems more so than lyric poems and narratives that don't necessarily tell a story, but which might suggest the narrative of a moment or a period of time. In a poem such as 'Dairy Farmers at the Beach' I began by trying to describe the image of my dairy farming parents standing on a beach in their farming clothes marvelling at the water which appeared to be so foreign to them and how out of touch they were with a beach culture many Australians assume to be universal. That the poem developed into a portrait of a family leaving the beach to milk cows on an afternoon in the south-west of Victoria was a narrative that I hadn't planned or imagined. And yet, I always wanted to write about the three N towns that I grew up near—Naringal, Nullawarre and Nirranda—towns that were located on the Great Ocean Road inland from the beach town of Peterborough. Many poets that I have enjoyed explore the narrative form and the list in my head varies but it may include: Wordsworth, Seamus Heaney, Philip Levine, Elizabeth Bishop, Martin Harrison, Les Murray, C K Williams, Charles Wright, perhaps Phillip Hodgins. On the other hand, there are many other poets that I return to that might write a mix of narrative and lyrical poetry such as Sharon Olds, Sylvia Plath, Sinead Morrissey, Robert Gray, Robert Adamson, Sarah Holland Batt etc. The list is thankfully endless. Writing poetry doesn't make much money but for me it has always been an immersive process to be thinking about poetry each day. For me, it has also helped to have a full-time day job to create the tension necessary to write and naturally there are weeks when there is no poetry being written, yet poems may still be read, ruminated on or read about.

As mentioned earlier, I have included 30 new poems in the collection, poems which I imagine extend some of the concerns of my earlier collections. One notable feature of the new poems is that a number of them were written after my father died in October 2024. Frank Ryan, was an influence upon my writing in many ways, not least through his presence in my early poems as the farmer I often wrote about. This wasn't always a deliberate tactic on my behalf, often it was because he was actually in the scene that I was writing about such as in 'A breather' or 'The blessing'. At times, in some early poems, my father was a presence or voice to rail against, to depict or show. In later years, his presence was one for me to empathise with, and to illuminate through his many laconic and at times poetic sayings. These final poems seek to capture some of the concerns and thoughts of my father for myself and my brothers and sisters while we cared for him at home in the final stages of health conditions brought on by gradual heart failure. As anybody who has cared for a parent, friend or relative in the stages of dying knows, it can be a fraught, emotional and bonding experience. To write poems out of such an experience can be therapeutic, but for me it felt necessary. Writing poems has often been a way for me to make sense of the world around me, even more so when my father was dying.

The title, *What it Feels Like*, for this volume came early in the process. I was looking for a poem that held some of my ongoing concerns as well as a poem that represented some of my style or way of addressing a reader. 'What it feels like' is a list poem, written in couplets, using a basic, repetitive anaphora of 'It is' to create a slightly negative view of life in the country. I remember one initial idea for the poem was to write in response to people I knew in the city who would often ask me what it was like to grow up in the country. Perhaps my style was more direct then. I remember I wanted to encapsulate a feeling of living in the country by finding a line or image that remained with the reader. Many of the lines in the poem were taken from descriptions of people that I knew or had observed. These lines gave the poem its authenticity and perhaps impact. Authenticity, real descriptions of life, poetic truths and poems that remain with you are the poems I have always been drawn to. I hope that you find some such poems in this collection.

# Notes

1. The poem 'Why I am not a farmer' was inspired by the poem, 'Why I am not a painter', Frank O'Hara, *The Collected Poems of Frank O'Hara*, University of California Press, 1995
2. The poem 'Travelling through the family' was inspired by a Carlos Drummond De Andrade poem 'Travelling in the family' trans. Elizabeth Bishop in *The Complete Poems of Elizabeth Bishop: 1927-1979*, Farrar, Strauss and Giro, 1979
3. In the poem 'Heifer wearing a fencepost' the phrase 'aversion therapy' was taken from the short story,'Kill or Cure' Cate Kennedy, *Dark Roots*, Scribe.
4. 'Home': this poem was set in the remote Indigenous community of Ampilawatja, N.T and was partially inspired by a reading of *Journey to Horseshoe Bend*, TGH Strehlow, Giramondo Classics, 2015.
5. The following lines are taken from the book:
    'Thy Will be Done,' p213.
    'the man regarded as a rock, beginning to crumble' p213.
6. The poem 'Feldspar' is based on the Hazards mountain range overlooking Coles Bay in Tasmania where the feldspar granite is flecked with iron oxide impurities and which renders the stony sides of the mountain range pink in the afternoon sun.
7. 'Taking It Slow': Aradale was a psychiatric hospital in Ararat, Vic. and sometimes it was referred to as the Aradale Lunatic Asylum. It operated from 1867-1993.
8. Midnight Oil and Goanna played at Mt Duneed outside Geelong on March 5, 2022.

New Poems

1. 'Dreams a daughter lets slip': The final line of the poem was inspired by the last lines of Philip Larkin's The Whitsun Weddings:
    'like an arrow-shower
    sent out of sight, somewhere becoming rain.'

2. 'Joan Eardley': Joan Eardley was an English-born artist who lived much of her life in Glasgow and Catterline, a small village on the east coast of Scotland. The poem was inspired by a reading of Elliot, Patrick, *Joan Eardley: Land & Sea—A life in Catterline*, (2021) National Galleries of Scotland, Edinburgh
3. The line 'the War still on' in the poem 'Archway' is taken from the diary of Rose La Fontaine, (unpublished) and refers to World War Two continuing.
4. The title of the poem 'There There' was taken from the Radiohead song of the same name.
5. UDV (United Dairy farmers of Victoria) refers to newspaper clippings that my father kept through is involvement in the union.

# Acknowledgments

Grateful thanks to the publishers of my previous books of poetry and memoir: Ron Pretty, *Five Islands Press*, Anthony Lynch, *Whitmore Press*, John Hunter, *Hunter Publishers,* Ralph Wessman, *Walleah Press* and Shane Strange, *Recent Work Press*.

Heartfelt thanks to the many editors of newspapers and literary journals where poems in this collection were first published. The following new poems were first published in the following journals:
'Inheritance', *Island*
'Roaming'*, Australian Poetry Anthology*, Vol. 11, 2024
'The snaking accuracy of cow trails', 2024 Newcastle Poetry Prize shortlist
'Weather' and 'Joan Eardley', *Stylus Lit*
'Finding pieces of my father', *The Australian*

A big thank you to the following people who have read and provided feedback on poems in the collection: Anne Gleeson, Phillip Hall, Shane Strange, Charlie, Lucinda and Alison Girvan.

# About the author

Brendan Ryan grew up on a dairy farm at Panmure in Western Victoria. His poetry, reviews and essays have been widely published in literary journals and newspapers. His second collection of poetry, *A Paddock in his Head* was shortlisted for the 2008 ACT Poetry Prize and his fourth collection, T*ravelling Through the Family* was shortlisted for the 2014 Victorian Premier's Prize for Poetry. His poetry collection, *The Lowlands of Moyne* was Highly Commended in the 2020 Wesley Michel Wright Poetry Prize. The recipient of three Writer's Grants from The Australia Council, his poems have been shortlisted for the Peter Porter Poetry Prize, The Newcastle Poetry Prize and the ACU Poetry Prize. His memoir, *Walk Like a Cow*, was published in 2020 with Walleah Press. He lives in Geelong, Victoria where he is the Library Manager at a secondary college.

www.ingramcontent.com/pod-product-compliance
Lightning Source LLC
Chambersburg PA
CBHW060556080526
44585CB00013B/588